The Gardener's Book of
Heathers

Geoffrey Yates

FREDERICK WARNE

Published by Frederick Warne (Publishers) Ltd, London, 1985

Cover picture, *Winter-flowering Heaths*, supplied by
Harry Smith Horticultural Photographic Collection.

ISBN Limp 0 7232 3166 4
ISBN Cased 0 7232 3193 1

Printed and bound in Great Britain by William Clowes Limited
Beccles and London

2

Contents

Acknowledgements

However much a book of this type is built on the experience and researches of the author, it also inevitably owes much to the work, comments and advice of other people. My own pleasure in growing heathers has been increased, and my specialist knowledge widened, by reading a number of books on the subject, and in some cases I have had the privilege of meeting the authors. To them, and to members of the Heather Society, encountered especially at some of the early Northern Group meetings (held at Harrogate), I owe a great debt for the wealth of experience and knowledge they were willing to share. I have also been able to travel fairly extensively, and have learnt much from those in Holland and Germany, as well as in Britain, who share my interests.

I have always enjoyed the full support of my wife and family. I would also like to thank the staff at Warne's who have helped me to expand my Pocket Guide, which has been in print for thirteen years, into this larger book that I feel the subject now thoroughly deserves.

Most of the illustrations I have provided myself, but I should like to acknowledge with thanks the loan of transparencies by Kurt Kramer, P. G. Turpin, Curt Brose and Hermann Westermann. Photographs on pages 52, 57, 65, 69, 92, 105 and 138 are reproduced by permission of A–Z Botanical Collection Ltd.; those on pages 47, 48, 73, 83, 84, 85, 87, 89, 91, 109, 112, 119 and 131 by permission of Photos Horticultural. I would like to thank R. B. Davis for the use of his drawings of heather species. I am indebted to David McClintock for his help with the Index; to Chris Brickell for his foreword; to all others who have replied to my queries about cultivars and also to owners of gardens who have allowed pictures of their gardens to be used.

Geoffrey Yates
January 1984

Foreword

The tremendous rise in the popularity of heathers as garden plants during the last twenty years has resulted partly from their versatility and ease of cultivation and partly from the extraordinary variation in flower and foliage colour exhibited by the very small percentage of the 600 or so known species that are recognized by botanists.

The Heather Society, formed in 1963, has played a very large part in encouraging gardeners to use heathers in a wide range of diverse climates and different garden situations—even as window box or tub plants for those unfortunate enough to live in houses or flats lacking gardens. Equally important has been the willingness of specialist nurserymen to make available and maintain stocks of large numbers of cultivars that have inevitably resulted from the increased interest in heathers. Sadly, not all the introductions are distinct or horticulturally worthwhile; but a visit to a large heather garden, such as that at Harlow Car, Windsor Great Park or Wisley, at any season of the year will convince the unconverted on their value as garden plants.

Geoffrey Yates has been a heather enthusiast for many years. His wide knowledge, based on his personal experience of growing heathers in Britain and studying them throughout Europe, has been made readily available to the increasing numbers of gardeners growing heathers through his *Pocket Guide to Heathers* first published in 1968 and last revised in 1978. The inclusion in this work of a very comprehensive list of names of heather cultivars, in effect an outline International Register of cultivar names for heathers, was a major step forward in stabilising the naming of this group.

The expansion of Geoffrey Yates' classic pocket book into the present volume will be much welcomed by heather enthusiasts. It is particularly pleasing that the author and publishers have maintained the formidable but most important index to heather names in this volume, an invaluable reference for use until the long awaited International Register of heather names is published by the Heather Society.

I am sure that all gardeners interested in heathers and many yet to be introduced to this beautiful group of plants will benefit greatly from the detailed and accurate information provided by Mr Yates in this book.

C D Brickell
Director, RHS Gardens, Wisley
29.7.83

Introduction

Heaths and heathers are among the most interesting groups of plants found in gardens today. But unfortunately, as public interest has increased, so has the flood of 'new' names available in garden centres and nurseries. This has caused considerable confusion. I have tried to keep pace with new introductions by growing them myself or observing them elsewhere, and by comparing them with already established and popular cultivars. In order to include some of them it has been necessary, over a period of thirteen years, for me to revise my *Pocket Guide to Heather Gardening* three times. I now feel that the time is ripe to publish an illustrated guide that will give both the newcomer and the enthusiast some chance to see what each group of cultivars has to offer in terms of colour and interest. I plan to list as many as possible of the cultivars currently available at the time of going to press.

Of the large number of 'new' cultivars introduced in recent years, comparatively few are distinct, or even appreciably different, from one or other of the cultivars already available. Some are improvements of existing forms; some, similar in colour and habit, flower rather earlier or later. But the majority are of no commercial or horticultural significance. Often a 'new' cultivar has been introduced by an enthusiast or nurseryman who, because he or she lacks knowledge of the very wide selection already produced, genuinely believes it to be totally new and different.

This problem of the multiplicity of 'new' cultivars is in process of being sorted out. The Heather Society, as the international registration authority, has a prime duty to see that names are not duplicated and that use of discontinued names is abandoned. To this end it maintains a register, in the constant reorganization of which considerable progress has been made in integrating and recoding 'new' cultivars. But ultimately a complete register must depend on the establishment of a sufficient number of full reference collections, so that nurserymen and specialist growers may compare their new seedlings and sports. A first step in this task was taken when a group of enthusiasts set up a comprehensive, carefully catalogued collection at Harlow Car Gardens, Harrogate, a few years ago. Information thus acquired formed the basis of a report published by the Heather Society (1976), and also gave rise to the compilation of the Society's Colour Chart, against which all heather flower colours should now be classified.

Harlow Car Gardens, however, have not the space for the maintenance of a permanent complete collection, and another site or sites must be sought. At the moment, the most complete heather collections in the United Kingdom are in private hands. The most

The trial of double flowered and foliage Callunas at Rostrup

comprehensive collection I have ever seen is in Germany, maintained at the Horticultural Research Station, Rostrup, Bad Zwischenahn; despite severe damage in the hard winter of 1981–82 it is still excellent. In Holland, I understand that the main collections suffered very badly and will take some time to recover.

In this book I, also, have had to deal with the not yet totally resolved problem posed by the many so-called 'new' cultivars. My choice of which ones to illustrate, which is inevitably individual and implies no automatic criticism of those I omit, is based on my own experience and observation. Some cultivars that I appear to have relegated to a secondary status could easily have featured as my first choice; others have distinctive characteristics that perhaps make them less generally suitable although highly to be recommended for particular situations.

Such factors I have noted.

But in order to provide as full as possible a list, not only of the hardy heathers, but also of all cultivar names whether or not still available, I have compiled a comprehensive index. In this the reader will find all cultivar names listed alphabetically under the original hardy species from which they derive. Symbols will indicate further details, such as those names that are now obsolescent, whereas a page reference will take the reader to the place in the book where an available cultivar is described (and either the cultivar itself, or one very similar is illustrated).

I have, of necessity, made rather broad each group into which I have arranged a number of cultivars, so that within it some variations occur in habit of growth, height, foliage, colour and vigour. Within a fairly narrow range flower colour and flowering time will also vary; but, in general, plants of the same basic colour have been placed together, although some will be pale and others deep. It is even more difficult to group certain delicate colours, because pink and red flowers in heathers always have a certain amount of blue in them, and the amount of this can make a colour vary from pink to mauve. In other cultivars a complete flowering head or those of a group of plants appear different in colour from a single floret; my colour classification of these has been according to overall appearance.

I have not explained the origins of the various cultivars, except in order to illustrate a point of general interest. This is because the Heather Society's International Register, which should be published before too long, will give more detailed and comprehensive information than I could possibly include, and should satisfy all those wishing to study the plants' history in depth. Nor have I cited awards given to various heathers, because they are too closely related to local conditions, and so can be misleading in a book designed for widespread use.

Heather Species and Natural Hybrids

The heaths and heathers grown in gardens belong to a very large family, Ericaceae, and the particular genera with which we are concerned are *Erica, Calluna* and *Daboecia*, but only the hardy species amongst them. Out of the *Erica* genus, 630 or so are Cape Heathers and not hardy for outside use in Northern Europe. The natural distribution of the hardy species is almost entirely confined to European soil.

All hardy heaths and heathers are found growing naturally on treeless, open landscapes in full sun and open air. The natives of the British Isles and northern Europe can be found in any similar conditions at heights varying from sea-level to over 61 m (200 ft). They flourish in a wide variety of soils, but not in those containing lime. *Erica cinerea*, the Bell Heather, favours drier, stony slopes, *Erica tetralix*, the Cross-leaved Heath, the wetter peat bogs, and *Calluna vulgaris*, Ling, intermediate moorlands. The other species native to Britain are more localized, *Erica vagans*, the Cornish Heath, being confined to Cornwall and parts of Ireland, and *Erica ciliaris*, the Dorset Heath, to Dorset, with small areas in Cornwall, Devon and southwest Ireland. *Erica erigena* is prolific in a very small area of western Ireland, and also grows in northern Spain and in a small area in southern France around the shores of the Bay of Biscay.

Erica scoparia, the Besom Heath, is hardy but rarely grown in gardens, as the flowers are uninteresting; it grows over large areas of southern France, Spain and around the Mediterranean. The popular name arises from its use in France to make besoms.

The Corsican Heath, *Erica terminalis*, from Corsica, Sardinia, southern Italy and south-western Europe, is regarded as a tree heath in cultivation because it grows into a substantial shrub; and, despite its native habitat, it is quite hardy in Britain.

The true Tree Heath, *Erica arborea*, grows extensively on dry, rocky hillsides in countries bordering the Mediterranean extending east to the Caucasus and, in North Africa, covering large tracts of ground and reaching treelike proportions. It flowers from mid-winter until spring. The roots are used for making tobacco pipes, its name in France being *bruyère* which is corrupted to 'briar'; it is also an important source of fuel. In Spain a hardier form grows at elevations of more than 1219 m (4000 ft), and this is the source of a form in cultivation known as *Erica arborea* 'Alpina'.

Another popular tree heath in garden cultivation is *Erica australis*. This is hardy in most of Britain, although it can be badly damaged by heavy snowfalls. It grows naturally on hillsides in Portugal and southwest Spain, and forms part of the flora of that area along with *Erica lusitanica*, another tall heath which flowers early in the year. This species has naturalized itself in southwest England and is prolific.

Erica carnea is undoubtedly one of the most useful species owing to the masses of colour it brings to our gardens in winter; and its tolerance in growing well in most soils and situations is an added bonus. The natural home of this species is at high levels in the central European Alps, hence its natural hardiness.

Erica mackaiana is a species much less well-known, but a most attractive one, occurring rarely in northwest Ireland and northwest Spain. The garden forms are, justifiably, becoming more popular.

Much less frequently grown in gardens, but still fairly hardy despite its Portuguese origin, *Erica umbellata* is a charming plant with beautiful mauve flowers appearing in April to June when there is very little else blooming in a heather garden. It grows well on alkaline soils, preferably well drained. Its natural habitat spreads across Portugal, southwest Spain and Morocco.

The last of the true species are the Daboecias. *Daboecia cantabrica*, or St Daboec's Heath, found on the moors in Co. Mayo and Co. Galway, and in northern Spain, Portugal and southwest France, can be cut back in hard winters, but invariably recovers well and quickly. It has proved to be drought tolerant and to grow on alkaline soils in cultivation.

Daboecia azorica is native only to the Azores and the true species is not reliably hardy in northern Europe. Fortunately it has passed on its dwarf habit and the red colouring to the popular hybrids *Daboecia x scotica*. Most plants in cultivation under the name of the species are hybrids, although the true species is still grown from seed collected at high altitudes.

In addition to the species already mentioned, a number of hybrids have been found in the wild and are excellent garden plants. A hybrid is a plant produced when one species crosses with another by pollen from one fertilizing the stigma of a member of a different species. When different species grow in close proximity, it is inevitable that hybrid forms will be produced, and these provide much food for thought for botanists in deciding whether they are hybrids or new species, and what name should be given to them. Such hybrids are more often than not sterile, which means that unless they are brought into cultivation and propagated vegetatively, they soon die out.

Erica x *praegeri* is named after the original finder of the first plant discovered growing from a cross between *Erica mackaiana* and *Erica tetralix*. Different forms collected from different sites have provided some excellent garden plants. The parentage is established by scientific means. It has now been re-classified as *Erica* x *stuartii*.

Erica x *veitchii* is a hybrid tree heath originating as a chance cross between *Erica arborea* and *Erica lusitanica* in Veitch's Nursery, Exeter, before 1905.

Most of the crosses in the group *Erica* x *watsonii* now grown in cultivation have come from the 'Great Heath' near Wareham in Dorset, where both *Erica ciliaris* and *Erica tetralix* grow and have produced many good forms. These have been collected by the owners and staff of the famous heather nursery of Maxwell & Beale in Dorset; all have the foliage and flowers of *Erica ciliaris*, and height and long flowering period of *Erica tetralix*.

Erica x *williamsii*, a hybrid between *Erica vagans* and *Erica tetralix*, has produced only two named clones, both collected on the Lizard Peninsula in Cornwall.

The name of the winter-flowering hybrids *Erica* x *darleyensis* is applied to various well-known cultivated forms all originating as seedlings in gardens as a result of *Erica erigena* crossing with *Erica carnea*. The first of such hybrids arose at Darley Dale in Derbyshire; all are very hardy and tolerant of most soils and situations.

The most recently named group is *Daboecia* x *scotica*, the name given to hybrids between *Daboecia azorica* and *Daboecia cantabrica*, the cultivated forms of which are very popular low-growing plants.

Garden Forms and their Names

In summarizing the distribution in the wild of the various heather species, it will be apparent that there are many unanswered questions as to how such distribution came about, and what is the relationship between populations of the same species existing both in southern Europe and in the western counties of Ireland. These puzzles can be explained only by reference to factors existing long before the formation of the present land masses of the northern hemisphere. We do know that there was sufficient interest in heathers as well as other plants for records to be made in the sixteenth century, and in 1770

Linnaeus recorded 23 species of *Erica*, some from the Cape. By the early eighteenth century over 400 species were in cultivation and it was the height of fashion to grow them. Naturally, most of these were Cape Heaths, grown in glasshouses, or in a conservatory, but as with all fashions the enthusiasm died out, and it was only towards the end of the nineteenth century that interest in hardy heathers was reawakened.

While it is difficult to trace the origins of some heathers still cultivated in gardens, the histories of others are well known, and intelligent speculation about many others provides us with satisfactory answers. The development of the wide choice we have today is a permanent memorial to a long line of very delightful and dedicated plant lovers. These had the skill and judgement to recognize a beautiful new plant, seen either somewhere in the wild, and perhaps surrounded by more ordinary species, or as a seedling coming up by chance in some garden or nursery.

Many of the old introductions are still unsurpassed today, despite the flood of new ones in recent years. Originally, in order to be regarded as 'worthwhile', a plant had to be distinct from, or superior to anything already known. By the time the Heather Society, as the International Registration Authority, publishes the Register in the near future, all the known origins will be recorded; but this useful authentification will fortunately not diminish the pleasure to be had from reading many of the more amusing and interesting stories in books mentioned in previously published literature.

Heathers in the Garden

Heathers in a garden need by no means be restricted to a heather garden. The claim that they will provide 'colour all the year round' is fully justified, because many heather cultivars can be used in association with other plants and shrubs as part of an overall scheme. The golden rule to bear in mind is that for best results heaths and heathers must be grown fully exposed to sun and wind, as they all originate from a natural environment of hills, moorland, or open, exposed places. However, they will grow in less favoured situations, but cannot be expected to excel in adversity.

Conditions to be avoided are total shade, places where heathers will be swamped by larger, vigorous plants or where the foliage will be covered by falling leaves. Heathers look after themselves very well in relation to most competitors, but there are limits to their ability to grow. Many people imagine that heathers will thrive in difficult places where nothing else will grow. While there are, indeed, some situations where this is true, total shade, or areas under dense trees, or wet, boggy ground do not come within this category. There are other plants more suitable for these situations and the nurseryman would not wish the plants he has so carefully raised and nurtured to be consigned to a life of misery in totally unsuitable conditions.

Soil Conditions   All plants respond differently to varying soil conditions, but unlike most other plants heathers produce best results in soil that would normally be classed as poor. This is easy to understand if their natural environment is considered. Natural habitat is always the perfect clue as to where any garden plant should be grown, but because of our enthusiasm to grow plants from all over the world it is only on the rare occasion that ideal conditions can be provided. Fortunately, heathers of the hardy species can be more easily accommodated than most. Moorland soil is normally well-drained loam containing a large amount of natural humus formed over many years by decaying vegetation. This humus is its important feature, because heathers prefer lime-free soil, and the presence of decaying humus always increases soil acidity. Heathers can often be found growing in humus-filled pockets overlying limestone rocks, but in such conditions the roots keep in the shallow acid layers of humus, leaving the plants exposed to summer drought, winter frosts and other adverse conditions, with the result that the plants are not totally at ease.

Soil texture is more important than any other factor in the successful growing of heathers. No species will thrive on stiff, cold, adhesive clay more the texture of plasticine, as the fine hairy roots cannot penetrate this medium; the most important step is to ensure a well-drained, open medium by incorporating stones, gravel, half-rotted lime-free compost, old straw, or similar material. Peat, unless it is coarse and lumpy, does very little to improve clay soils and it is too far advanced in decomposition to be long lasting. Coarse, lime-free grit is far more beneficial than peat as an addition to soil; peat or pulverized bark can be applied as a top dressing and will encourage worms to do the digging for you, and improve the soil texture in the way that nature intended.

Alkaline and Mineral Deficient Soils   It is generally assumed that plants belonging to the Ericacae (which includes all heaths and heathers) will not grow on soils containing lime. Lime is normally measured in the form of a 'pH' number, and a scale is used by gardeners to show the degree of acidity or alkalinity. As the diagram shows, pH 7 is neutral, and in theory no attempt should be made to grow ericaceous plants in soil above a pH 6. Simple soil test kits can be purchased, or your heather nurseryman will test your soil for you if you are in doubt.

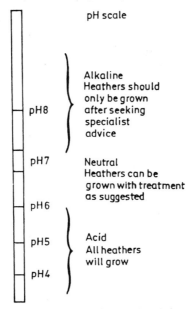

pH scale

pH8 { Alkaline
Heathers should
only be grown
after seeking
specialist
advice

pH7 Neutral
Heathers can be
grown with treatment
as suggested

pH6

pH5 { Acid
All heathers
will grow

pH4

In practice, the actual structure of the soil and the type of lime in it is more important than the pH reading, as heaths and other ericaceous plants can be found growing on top of limestone where the pH reading may be as high as 8. The reasons for this are that magnesium or dolomitic limestone is not harmful, whereas calcium as found on chalk outcrops is.

Soils with a high pH reading are usually unsuitable because of a deficiency of iron, magnesium and manganese; these deficiencies can be overcome by treating the soil with a trace element additive generally sold as Fritted Trace Elements. Plants need these trace elements in only very small quantities, and a little goes a long way. Treatment with Sequestrene is another popular method, but this is more expensive and short term in its effects. The use of Fritted Trace Elements is much more satisfactory, and restores health to sickly hydrangeas, camellias and rhododendrons as well as to heathers. I have carried out trials for many years, treating soils with high calcium content (in one case reaching a pH of 8·5); all the ericaceous plants grew successfully in the treated soil. I must emphasize that the texture of the soil is vital to success, and the addition of plenty of humus as advised under the section on cultivation is most important. The rotting down process of all forms of humus lowers pH and provides the trace elements so vital to ericaceous plants. With most plants, poor growth, lack of flowers, yellowing of foliage and other symptoms normally indicate the need for additional fertilizer such as nitrogen or potash. But with ericaceous plants these symptoms more often signify a lack of trace elements.

I certainly would not advise anyone to start planting a large heather garden in totally unsuitable soil conditions such as the high pH soils found in the Cotswolds or in southeast England. Nevertheless, it is always worthwhile to look further into the problem; many gardeners may be able to change the conditions sufficiently to make ericaceous plants happy without the labour and expense of removing existing soil and importing some more suitable.

The Use of Heathers in Mixed Plantings   The basic needs of heathers have been mentioned. Suggestions now follow for growing them in various parts of the garden such as mixed beds or borders. The winter-flowering *Erica carnea, Erica* x *darleyensis* and *Erica erigena* cultivars are ideal as they provide colour at a time of year when very few other plants do so. Also, they will give the maximum return for the minimum amount of attention whether in association with other garden plants, in window-boxes, tubs, troughs or in pots. (By mentioning pots, I do not suggest using the plants for growing in the house, although winter-flowering cultivars grown in pots outside can be taken indoors to flower, provided they are taken outside again for growing on for another year.)

I have grown *Erica carnea* cultivars in tubs along with dwarf rhododendrons, dwarf conifers and azaleas, and they have flowered freely and grown well for many years in return for a light dressing of a slow-release organic fertilizer. Summer-flowering cultivars can also be used in the same way, but there is a wider choice of other plants to provide summer colour, and people often prefer to use bedding plants. If heathers are used, these can be cheaper over a period of a few years.

·Where heathers are used in association with other plants, it is important to use cultivars of a size similar to that of the companion plants. The choice ranges from those 5 cm (2 in) high to 150 cm (5 ft), and within each range of sizes the variation in foliage, flower colour, flowering times and general habit is considerable. Where a tub, trough, or window-box is being planted, a heather of considerable vigour will very quickly dominate slower growing ones. In the same way, if heathers are used in a rockery alongside alpines, it is necessary to select heathers of similar vigour. There are many very dwarf cushion heathers and slow-growing cultivars that grow quite happily with slow, dwarf alpines, but it is important that they are not planted alongside vigorous alpines such as Aubretia, Phlox, Alyssum and Campanulas, as the dwarf heathers would be swamped and very quickly spoilt.

Heathers form an important part of a mixed border or shrubbery, as the choice of heather cultivars which flower at different times of the year will much extend the flowering season. It is vital that the larger, stronger-growing cultivars are used, in order to keep them in scale with the remainder of the planting.

Winter-flowering heathers make attractive edgings to beds of summer-flowering plants such as roses. They provide colour during the dormant season of the roses, when the beds look bare. If they are planted as an edging, they do not interfere with the heavy feeding programme needed to keep the roses in good condition. For some years I grew lilies in a bed covered with heathers, and the lilies thrived with the protection of the established heathers, which in turn acted as an ideal foil for the lily flowers. Spring bulbs grow well if allowed to come up through a ground cover of summer- or winter-flowering heathers, and there are innumerable uses of this type. The major point to bear in mind is that in the case of plants needing heavy fertilizer and manure dressings, the heathers must only be used as an edging as they will not survive heavy feeding.

In almost any garden situation exposed to the sun for at least part of the day, and not totally overhung by trees, a bare patch can be transformed to an area of beauty in either summer or winter. Heathers chosen for their foliage colour alone will be attractive throughout the year and are especially useful where the surrounding plants shed their leaves in winter. *Erica cinerea* cultivars do best in drier conditions, *Erica tetralix* in damp areas and winter-flowering cultivars and *Erica vagans* on alkaline soils. There is a species of heather to suit all parts of the garden except for areas in complete shade.

Flower arrangers can find plenty of useful material, especially the double-flowered Callunas such as 'H. E. Beale', 'Elsie Purnell', 'Peter Sparkes', 'My Dream', with the very long flower spikes, and dwarf doubles 'County Wicklow', 'Kinlochruel' and others so ideal for small arrangements. Many of the cultivars grown for foliage effect have long, graceful stems, as do many single-flowered plants. There is scope for including some of these cultivars in a flower arranger's cutting border.

For the less sophisticated or ambitious arranger, the double-flowered Callunas cut just before the flower stem reaches its peak, will last throughout the winter if freshly cut stems are stuck into Oasis or an old potato. This type of arrangement rinsed under a cold water tap occasionally, to remove dust, will still be showing full colour when the next season's flowers start in the garden.

Designing a Heather Garden

A garden is such an individual reflection of its maker that it is impossible to lay down hard and fast rules for creating it. If we see a garden and immediately think it is beautiful, this is because it has some of the features or characteristics that we should wish to include. We can find a garden attractive because of its setting, the way it complements the house it surrounds, the trees and shrubs it contains, or one or two very minor features in it. Equally, what we should otherwise find attractive can be spoilt by one very simple feature which, to us, mars the whole effect.

The opportunities of seeing other people's gardens, both large and small, have never been greater, as there are now over 2,000 gardens open at various times of the year through charitable schemes such as The National Gardens Scheme, Scotland's Gardens Scheme, Gardener's Sunday, as well as The National Trust, The National Trust for Scotland and the Ulster Gardens Scheme. Many other gardens open on a regular basis. My advice to anybody designing a garden is to visit as many others as you can, see ideas that appeal to you, learn from the mistakes that others have made, and then sit down with pencil and paper and draw a rough plan. Nothing is more heartbreaking or wasteful in time, energy and money, than to plant a new garden in haste, and then, in a year or two, to have to pull something out that has grown too large, or is in the wrong place. By visiting other gardens you learn very quickly which plants, trees and shrubs you like, how big they will become, and how far apart they should be planted; visual instruction of this type is more valuable than any amount of reading.

If you take over an established garden, live with it for a year to see exactly what it contains. Think very seriously before removing established trees and shrubs; they have taken years to grow, and the minutes spent in mutilating or chopping them down may be regretted for years afterwards.

The use of heathers mixed with other garden features has already been mentioned. My aim now is to offer helpful ideas for making a heather garden, border, or bed which can comprise the entire garden, or be just a feature in it. Plantsmen, those who love growing plants for their individual qualities, will be more concerned with including as

The mosaic planting—groups of three or five or a single plant of each cultivar in a small area

many different cultivars as possible. They will ensure that the plants are given good growing conditions and the right situation in the garden, and that nearby species are compatible. I have seen many beautiful gardens made on this basis, and such is the variety in height, shape, foliage, colours and flowering times of the various heather species included, that the mosaic effect of such a garden, because it is always changing, takes a lot of beating.

The purist will always contend that heather moorlands are large drifts of the same species, and this type of planting is very effective in a large garden, especially if it is in a woodland or natural setting. A heather garden made up of big drifts of one cultivar is most effective, as can be seen in illustrations, and at the Royal Horticultural Society Garden at Wisley, the Royal Botanic Garden at Edinburgh, Harlow Car Garden at Harrogate, Kew Gardens, and in many other places.

A large choice of cultivars is available, and this makes it difficult for a gardener to make a selection for his garden. The suggestions I have made are intended to provide a combination of different cultivars that will give the maximum impact at certain times of the year. There are plenty of alternatives, and by referring to the Descriptive List, these can be readily found, if some of the names I mention on the plans cannot be obtained.

Informality is the keynote, but to get an effective display, groups of one cultivar are preferable to individual plants. Such groups cannot be arranged in narrow beds, less than 1 metre wide, and in such cases I recommend either making blocks of colour of one cultivar, or the mosaic planting mentioned on page 19. If you are making new beds or borders, and space is available, try to use the dimensions shown, with the suggested plans under the heading Designs for Effect (page 21), or make them even larger if space permits. If existing beds or borders are being changed over to heathers and it is not possible to increase the size or alter the shape of the beds, the suggestions can be adapted without loss of overall effect, provided that there is sufficient width.

Whether to include conifers or other shrubs with heathers is a matter for personal choice. I have made four gardens of my own over the years and tried most combinations. To me, some have been disasters, while other people have considered them to be successes. The most natural mixture is to use tree heathers as the focal points amongst the lower growing heathers, but my advice is to plant your heather beds and then decide whether you want to put conifers, rhododendrons, azaleas, dwarf shrubs, potentillas, brooms, tree heathers or anything else amongst them. Whatever you decide, do remember that your heathers will be with you for many years, given a little care and attention, and any other interplanting must be something that will not get too large and swamp the rest of the planting. Before interplanting, find out how big the intended tree or shrub will be in ten years' time and keep to the dwarfer types of the genera of your choice.

Winter colour, that occurring between December and March, is one of the unique benefits that a heather planting will give. For this reason, consider which parts of the garden are visible from windows and which are seen every day on leaving and returning home. Do not forget the housewife who must spend part of her day with a view from the kitchen window, or the house-bound who may have a particular view day-in day-out. A bold patch of colour, whether in the form of flowers or colourful foliage, can light up the most depressing of winter days, or summer ones for that matter. It is a continuously changing picture as heathers in bud have a different colour from that shown when open and foliage changes colour, but is always evergreen.

A dull winter's day—interest from shape and foliage

How Many Plants are Needed   In average growing conditions five plants per square metre, the equivalent of planting them 45 cm (18 in) apart, will give complete ground cover in three years, using cultivars of normal rate of growth; three plants per square metre, equivalent to planting them 75 cm (30 in) apart, will take five years to cover the same area. When planting for an overall effect, minimum groups of five of each cultivar are recommended, as the advantage of a square metre of one colour, especially in winter, can be easily imagined. These groups can be increased in size for larger gardens. Flower colours rarely clash, all being natural colours, but it is important to keep neighbouring groups in proportion as far as height and flowering times are concerned. For those wishing to make their own designs, my section The Heather Year (pages 25–28) will help by giving flowering times of a wide choice of cultivars throughout the year. The section Designs for Effect provides ready-made plans for beds of various shapes and sizes.

Designs for Effect   The designs following are planned to be interesting for the season indicated in each case, and the sizes can be varied to suit any size of garden, provided that the same proportions are maintained for irregularly shaped beds.

Shaping irregular beds often causes problems to many gardeners. The easiest method for making an attractive outline is to use a lawnmower to make the shape, as by putting pegs at each end of the proposed bed, and marking the width in the same way, the mower is then pushed or driven round the outside of the pegs following the approximate shape planned, and you will find that in this way gradual curves are formed, and this has the added advantage of knowing that it will always be possible to mow round the edge of the bed on one run rather than having to manhandle the mower round awkward angles or sharp curves.

A. Island Bed

Planted with five plants of each cultivar suggested, and one plant of each specimen (lettered) would be 4 m (13 ft) long and 1·5 m (5 ft) wide. A smaller bed using three plants of each (still with the three lettered plants) would be 2·5 m (8 ft) long and 1 m (3 ft) wide. ★ Indicates good foliage colour if grown in a sunny position.

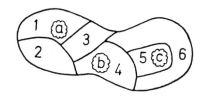

WINTER & SUMMER (any soil)

1. *E. carnea* 'King George'
2. *E. carnea* 'Foxhollow' ★
3. *E. vagans* 'Mrs D. F. Maxwell'
4. *E. carnea* 'Springwood White'
5. *E. x darleyensis* 'Jack H. Brummage' ★
6. *E. vagans* 'St Keverne'
a. *E. terminalis* 'Thelma Woolner'
b. *E. arborea* 'Alpina'
c. *Chamaecyparis lawsoniana* 'Ellwoodii'

SUMMER (acid soil only)

1. *E. tetralix* 'Pink Star'
2. *Calluna vulgaris* 'Robert Chapman' ★
3. *Calluna vulgaris* 'Peter Sparkes'
4. *E. cinerea* 'Knap Hill Pink'
5. *Calluna vulgaris* 'Beoley Gold' ★
6. *Calluna vulgaris* 'County Wicklow'
a. *Thuja occidentalis* 'Rheingold'
b. *Chamaecyparis pisifera* 'Boulevard'
c. *Chamaecyparis lawsoniana* 'Ellwoodii'

WINTER & SPRING (any soil)

1. *E. carnea* 'Vivellii'
2. *E. carnea* 'Myretoun Ruby'
3. *E. erigena* 'W. T. Rackliff'
4. *E. x darleyensis* 'Ada S. Collings'
5. *E. x darleyensis* 'Ghost Hills'
6. *E. carnea* 'Ann Sparkes' ★
a. *Thuja occidentalis* 'Rheingold' ★
b. *E. x darleyensis* 'Arthur Johnson'
c. *Juniperus stricta*

B. Island Bed

Planted with five plants of each would be 3 m (10 ft) in each direction, and the circular bed 2·5 m (8 ft) in diameter, and with three plants of each slightly less than 2·5 m (8 ft) and slightly less than 1·5 m (4 ft 9 in) respectively.

This design can be adjusted to make a round bed for the centre of a lawn or island site.

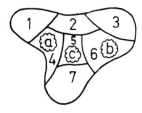

WINTER & SPRING (any soil)

1. *E. carnea* 'Foxhollow' ★
2. *E. carnea* 'Myretoun Ruby'
3. *E. carnea* 'March Seedling'
4. *E. carnea* 'Springwood White'
5. *E.* x *darleyensis* 'Furzey'
6. *E. carnea* 'December Red'
7. *E. carnea* 'Vivellii'
a. *E. erigena* 'Irish Dusk'
b. *E. erigena* 'W. T. Rackliff'
c. *E. arborea* 'Estrella Gold' ★

SUMMER & AUTUMN (acid soil)

1. *Calluna vulgaris* 'Golden Feather' ★
2. *E. cinerea* 'Pentreath'
3. *E. cinerea* 'Pink Ice'
4. *E. tetralix* 'Melbury White'
5. *Calluna vulgaris* 'Finale'
6. *E.* x *stuartii* 'Irish Lemon'
7. *E. vagans* 'St Keverne'
a. *Chamaecyparis laws.* 'Ellwood's Gold'
b. *Chamaecyparis pisifera* 'Boulevard'
c. *Chamaecyparis lawsoniana* 'Ellwoodii'

WINTER & SUMMER (acid soil)

1. *E. carnea* 'King George'
2. *E. vagans* 'Mrs D. F. Maxwell'
3. *E. cinerea* 'Golden Drop' ★
4. *Calluna vulgaris* 'Silver Queen' ★
5. *Calluna vulgaris* 'H. E. Beale'
6. *E. carnea* 'Vivellii'
7. *E. carnea* 'Springwood White'
a. *E. erigena* 'Superba'
b. *Juniperus stricta*
c. *Thuja occidentalis* 'Rheingold' ★

C. Border Bed (backed by path, hedge or fence)

Planted with five plants of each cultivar suggested, and one plant of each specimen (lettered) would be 4 m (13 ft) long and 1·5 m (4 ft

23

9 in) wide. A smaller bed using three plants of each (still with the three lettered plants) would be 2·5 m (8 ft) long and 1 m (3 ft) wide.

This design can be adapted to make a D-shaped bed for a more formal garden.

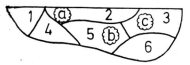

SUMMER & AUTUMN (acid soil)

1. *E. tetralix* 'Con Underwood'
2. *Calluna vulgaris* 'Peter Sparkes'
3. *Calluna vulgaris* 'Blazeaway' ★
4. *E. vagans* 'Mrs D. F. Maxwell'
5. *E. cinerea* 'Vivienne Patricia'
6. *Calluna vulgaris* 'Hibernica'
a. *Juniperus hibernica*
b. *Chamaecyparis pisifera* 'Filifera Aurea' ★
c. *Chamaecyparis lawsoniana* 'Allumii'

WINTER & SPRING (any soil)

1. *E. carnea* 'December Red'
2. *E. x darleyensis* 'Arthur Johnson'
3. *E. x darleyensis* 'Jack H. Brummage' ★
4. *E. carnea* 'Foxhollow' ★
5. *E. carnea* 'King George'
6. *E. carnea* 'Loughrigg'
a. *Chamaecyparis lawsoniana* 'Ellwoodii'
b. *Thuja occidentalis* 'Rheingold' ★
c. *Cham. lawsoniana* 'Columnaris Glauca'

WINTER & SUMMER (any soil)

1. *E. vagans* 'Lyonesse'
2. *E. x darleyensis* 'Jack H. Brummage' ★
3. *E. x darleyensis* 'Ghost Hills'
4. *E. carnea* 'Myretoun Ruby'
5. *E. vagans* 'St Keverne'
6. *E. carnea* 'Foxhollow' ★
a. *Chamaecyparis lawsoniana* 'Fletcheri'
b. *Chamaecyparis lawsoniana* 'Summer Snow'
c. *Thuja occidentalis* 'Rheingold'

D. Border Bed (rectangular shape)

Planted with five plants of each cultivar suggested, and one plant of each specimen (lettered) would be 4 m (13 ft) long and 1·5 m (4 ft 9 in) wide. A smaller bed using three plants of each (still with the three lettered plants) would be 2·5 m (8 ft) long and 1 m (3 ft) wide.

Informal shaped beds are strongly recommended but as many people wish to plant existing formal shaped beds without altering the garden the following suggestions are made:

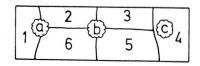

WINTER & SPRING (any soil)

1. *E. carnea* 'Foxhollow' ★
2. *E. x darleyensis* 'Furzey'
3. *E. carnea* 'King George'
4. *E. carnea* 'March Seedling'
5. *E. x darleyensis* 'Silberschmelze'
6. *E. carnea* 'Loughrigg'
a. *Chamaecyparis lawsoniana* 'Ellwoodii'
b. *E. australis* 'Riverslea'
c. *Juniperus stricta*

SUMMER & AUTUMN (acid soil)

1. *C. vulgaris* 'County Wicklow'
2. *E. cinerea* 'Pentreath'
3. *C. vulgaris* 'Sunset' ★
4. *C. vulgaris* 'Peter Sparkes'
5. *E. cinerea* 'Knap Hill Pink'
6. *E. tetralix* 'Hookstone Pink'
a. *Chamaecyparis pisifera* 'Filifera Aurea' ★
b. *Juniperus hibernica*
c. *Chamaecyparis lawsoniana* 'Summer Snow'

WINTER & SUMMER (any soil)

1. *E. vagans* 'Mrs D. F. Maxwell'
2. *E. carnea* 'King George'
3. *E. x darleyensis* 'Jack H. Brummage' ★
4. *E. carnea* 'Springwood White'
5. *E. erigena* 'Superba'
6. *E. vagans* 'Lyonesse'
a. *Juniperus hibernica*
b. *Thuja occidentalis* 'Rheingold' ★
c. *Chamecyparis pisifera* 'Boulevard'

The Heather Year

In order to assist the newcomer to choose suitable cultivars that will provide flowers throughout the year, I have set out below, under the different flowering seasons, a selection of the best cultivars. These have been chosen for reliability, good flowering, and for their attractiveness even when not in flower.

Flowering can vary by anything from three to six weeks from one geographical location to another. This applies especially to winter-flowering forms grown under different climatic conditions. Generally speaking, in early flowering areas cultivars in each group will be uniformly early, so a selection from each group will give the full year range. Unpruned summer-flowering cultivars will flower approximately two weeks earlier than those that have been clipped over. Many plants will overlap the flowering periods shown, but will start flowering in the period under which they are grouped.

Plants with unusually dwarf or slow growth, or those with extreme height or straggly growth have been excluded from the list. All species, therefore, except *Calluna vulgaris*, are comparable in size, and will never get out of place in most gardens. *Calluna vulgaris* has much more positive variation in habit, and for this reason I have given an alternative of low growing, compact or medium, and taller growing forms in each foliage or flower colour. Descriptions and illustrations of all the plants listed will be found between pages 36 and 139. (★ Indicates good foliage cover if grown in a sunny position.)

WINTER (December, January, February, March)

E. carnea 'King George' (pink)
E. carnea 'Springwood White' (white)
E. carnea 'R. B. Cooke' (lavender)
E. carnea 'December Red' (deep lilac-pink)
E. carnea 'Foxhollow' ★ (pale lavender)
E. carnea 'Ann Sparkes' ★ (deep rose-pink)
E. x *darleyensis* 'Arthur Johnson' (lilac-pink)
E. x *darleyensis* 'Ghost Hills' (pink)
E. x *darleyensis* 'Silberschmelze' (white)
E. carnea 'Loughrigg' (rose-pink)
E. carnea 'Pink Spangles' (pink/shell-pink bicolour)
E. carnea 'Myretoun Ruby' (deep heliotrope)
E. carnea 'Vivellii' (deep rose-pink)
E. x *darleyensis* 'Ada S. Collings' (white)

SPRING (March, April, May, June)

E. carnea 'March Seedling' (pale pink)
E. x *darleyensis* 'Furzey' (deep lilac-pink)
E. x *darleyensis* 'Jack H. Brummage' ★ (heliotrope)
E. erigena 'Irish Dusk' (salmon)
E. erigena 'W. T. Rackliff' (white)
E. erigena 'Brightness' (lilac-pink)
E. erigena 'Superba' (shell-pink)
E. umbellata (mauve)
Daboecia x *scotica* 'Tabramhill' (deep crimson)
Daboecia x *scotica* 'William Buchanan' (crimson)

Calluna vulgaris:

Colour	Low growing	Medium/Compact	Taller
Yellow spring growth	'Ruby Slinger'	'Kirby White'	'Spring Cream'
Orange, red, pink growth	'Leslie Slinger'	'Winter Chocolate'	'Fred J. Chapple'
		'Spring Torch'	'Spring Glow'

SUMMER (June, July, August, September)

E. tetralix 'Melbury White' (white)
E. tetralix 'Pink Star' (bright lilac-pink)
E. tetralix 'Con Underwood' (deep magenta)
Daboecia cantabrica 'David Moss' (white)
Daboecia cantabrica 'Hookstone Purple' (purple)
Daboecia cantabrica 'Praegerae' (deep pink)

E. cinerea 'Eden Valley' (lavender/white bicolor)
E. cinerea 'Miss Waters' (purple)
E. cinerea 'Glencairn' ★ (magenta)
E. cinerea 'Caldy Island' (amethyst)
E. cinerea 'White Dale' (white)
E. cinerea 'Stephen Davis' (magenta)
E. cinerea 'Plummers Seedling' (ruby)
E. cinerea 'Knap Hill Pink' (magenta)
E. cinerea 'Tom Waterer' (pale cerise)
E. cinerea 'Josephine Ross' (rose-pink)
E. cinerea 'Pentreath' (or 'Cindy') (beetroot)
E. cinerea 'Katinka' (or 'Ruby') (deep beetroot)
E. cinerea 'Rosea' (heliotrope)
E. cinerea 'Cevennes' (mauve)
E. cinerea 'Vivienne Patricia' (pale amethyst)
E. cinerea 'Ann Berry' ★ (amethyst)
E. cinerea 'Golden Drop' ★ (mauve)
Calluna vulgaris 'Calf of Man' (white)
E. x stuartii 'Irish Lemon' ★ (lilac-pink)
E. vagans 'Diana Hornibrook' (pale rose-pink)
E. ciliaris 'Mrs C. H. Gill' (crimson)
E. ciliaris 'Stoborough' (white)
E. ciliaris 'David McClintock' (white/pink)
E. ciliaris 'Corfe Castle' (rose-pink)

LATE SUMMER TO WINTER (August, September, October, November, December)

Calluna vulgaris:

Colour	Low growing	Medium/Compact	Taller
Double white	'Alba Plena'	'Kinlochruel'	'My Dream'
White	'Loch Turret'	'Drumra'	'Alba Elata'
Double rose or deep pink	'J. H. Hamilton'	'Cramond'	'Peter Sparkes'
Double shell-pink	'County Wicklow'	'Radnor'	'H. E. Beale'
			'Elsie Purnell'
			'Glencoe'
Crimson	'Alportii Praecox'	'Darkness'	'Beoley Crimson'
Very late flowering/mauve	'Hibernica'	'Johnson's Variety'	'Finale'

Daboecia cantabrica 'Lilacina' or 'Heather Yates' (amethyst)
E. vagans 'Mrs D. F. Maxwell' (deep rose-pink)
E. vagans 'St Keverne' (pink)
E. vagans 'Lyonesse' (white)
E. carnea 'Eileen Porter' (heliotrope)
E. carnea 'Jennifer Anne' (pale lilac-pink)

FOLIAGE PLANTS FOR ALL YEAR INTEREST

Calluna vulgaris

Foliage and flower colour	Low growing	Medium/Compact	Taller
Yellow/gold-white flowers	'Carole Chapman' 'Ruth Sparkes' (double)	'Harlequin' 'Beoley Gold'	'Serlei Aurea' 'Gold Haze'
Bronze foliage, lavender flowers	'Jenny'	'Inshriach Bronze'	'Cuprea'
Light orange foliage, lavender flowers	'Golden Carpet'	'Joy Vanstone'	'Orange Queen'
Orange foliage, turning copper-red in winter	'Multicolor' 'John F. Letts'	'Sir John Charrington' 'Sunset'	'Robert Chapman' 'Wickwar Flame'
Silver foliage, lavender flowers	'Sister Anne' 'Silver Cloud'	'Silver Queen' 'Silver Knight' 'Silver Rose' (superb in flower)	'Oxshott Common' 'Hirsuta Typica'
Silver/silver-grey foliage, white flowers		'Anthony Davis' 'Alison Yates' (more silver)	'Hirsuta Albiflora'

Cultivation

Soil Preparation   By describing the areas in which hardy heathers are found growing in the wild, the ideal soil conditions have been indicated. These comprise a crumbly loam with good drainage, acid in nature but not rich in plant foods. Very few people are fortunate enough to have gardens with this type of soil, but almost all soils will grow heathers successfully if a little trouble is taken when preparing them. Peat is not essential to the well-being of heathers. Well-drained soils containing a lot of stones or gravel are good conditions for heather, but they do benefit from the addition of moisture-retaining humus in the form of peat, pulverized bark, well-weathered sawdust or old garden compost that has not been treated with lime. Although I have gardened on soil of this sort for the past few years, I have found that such additional material is better used as a top dressing rather than incorporated with the soil before planting.

Light, sandy soils also need organic matter to help the retention of moisture; this can be added in the same way as for stony soil.

The greatest dislike of the heather family is solid clay, as mentioned earlier. This must be broken up by cultivation and the addition of lime-free grit or gravel, in order to allow the roots to wander freely through the soil.

Planting Time   So many plants are grown in pots or containers nowadays that we tend to regard any time as suitable for planting. While this is in the main true, I still prefer October, November, March and April, in that order. The greatest danger to newly planted heathers is that they will dry out, and this can happen just as easily as a result of severe frost and drying east winds in mid-winter, as it can with hot sun and drought in summer months.

Choose young, vigorous-looking plants. It is immaterial whether they are pot-grown or come from the open ground so long as they are well grown; a healthy root system is far more important than a large top to the plants. All too often, plants are grown under glass or in tunnels producing large, soft-textured plants which suffer disastrous consequences when exposed to the rigours of normal climate. The practice of forcing heathers to produce large plants in a short growing time appears to be confined to Britain, and I have been interested to see that in Germany and Holland plants are grown in open conditions, often on very exposed nurseries, and many in open ground beds. The quality of plants produced was better than most of these sold in Britain. However, many nurseries in Britain still produce excellent plants that have been grown slowly and are well hardened off to endure the weather conditions. These plants are the ones to look for, as they will best survive the winter, and by the early summer of the year after planting will have outgrown their soft-grown forced contemporaries, and all will have survived.

Although peat is not essential to healthy heathers, it is an excellent mulch, as is pulverized bark. It gives an attractive background for the newly planted heathers and deters weeds in newly cultivated ground. Obtain a few bags of either, put a layer on the surface 5 cm (2 in) thick and then plant through this top dressing. As you plant, enough will be incorporated in the soil to improve the texture round the newly planted roots.

Heathers should always be planted below the level of the soil mark on the plant stem, so that no free stem is exposed and the foliage is firmly seated on the ground. This hastens the establishment of the plants, as they will root along the stems that are in, or firmly embedded on the ground. Plants should not be trodden in as this will spoil all the good work done in preparing the ground to give it a nice spongy texture. Firm the plants in by hand and ensure that no air pockets are left round the root-ball.

After-care and Feeding   Once correctly planted, in well-cultivated soil, the main danger to heathers is drought and physical damage in the early months. Their root systems are shallow and the benefit of top dressing in the way advised is obvious. New plantings should be kept watered during dry spells in the first year, but this should not be done by frequent light waterings which encourage the root system to grow near to the surface. In a dry spell, a very thorough soaking every week or so will be more successful.

Traditionally, heathers have not been given fertilizer, as it is assumed to be unnecessary. In nature the breakdown of plant material on the surface of the ground provides sufficient nutrition, but in a tidy garden leaves and other dead plant material are usually removed, thereby disturbing the natural life-cycle of plant feeding. Heathers certainly benefit from modest applications of organic fertilizers such as bone meal, hoof and horn meal, seaweed, fish manure and John Innes base mixture at a rate of 50 grams ($1\frac{3}{4}$ oz) per square metre. Poor soils frequently suffer from deficiencies in minor elements such as iron, magnesium, copper, boron, cobalt, zinc, manganese and molybdenum, which are vital to the health of heathers. Steps taken to remedy this deficiency frequently help more than normal feeding. The methods of doing this are very important and can enable heathers to be grown on alkaline soils. I have set out full details on page 15.

Pruning   Trimming is a more accurate term for the annual treatment that should be given to heathers. Only the faded blooms should be cut away from the plant, just before new growth begins in the early spring; March or early April is the ideal time to do the work, and it is easy to see when this has been done consistently as the plants maintain a neat, bushy shape. Plants not treated in this way seem to lose vitality very quickly, are inclined to become ragged, and eventually the more vigorous forms become unmanageable.

The word pruning to me infers using secateurs or even a saw to cut back strong, straggly growths that have become totally out of hand. To help those who have neglected their heathers for a few years or taken over a neglected garden, a few words of advice on renovation of old plants may be useful. The bare woody stems, so prominent in old heathers, are the old flowering wood, which is the weakest part of the plant. This would have been removed if the trimming recommended had been carried out. This wood must be cut away in order to encourage new growth to develop below the old flower stems. If the plant has been neglected for too long, the new growth may have died out lower down the plant, and the remaining hard, woody stem will not produce young side growths. However, it is usually possible to find a few shoots growing from the base of the plant, and by cutting back all the old growth, leaving only the new young shoots, feeding and top dressing the plants as advised before, an old plant will soon recover.

The main problems arise with old, overgrown plants that show no signs of life at the base or lower down. In these cases it is really only a matter of patience and luck, as to whether plants can be restored to good condition. Unless you are very patient, my advice is, if in doubt, rip the plants out and start again. Once you have decided to try the restoration it must be done in easy stages. Remembering that heathers rarely make new growths from old, hard wood, the first cutting must be as low as possible without actually going below existing green growths; feed and top dress with a peaty soil mixture and then wait. After several months, new growth will have been made, and if the cutting back has encouraged breaks lower down the stem, you are in luck, and can cut even lower. In this way, over a period of two growing seasons, the plants can be improved.

The drastic alternative that does work is to dig up an old plant with as much soil intact as possible, and replant it deep enough to bury all the woody stems, leaving only the young, new foliage showing above the surface. Naturally there is a large element of risk in disturbing old plants in this way, but it is useful when one is anxious to retain a particular plant. If the moved plant is not allowed to dry out between lifting and replanting, it should eventually sprout. If this problem arises with low-growing plants, cut away the dead branches. Top dress the gaps with a peaty soil mixture and feed as before; the plant will soon recover and fill in the open parts with new growth.

Mulching or Top Dressing The main purpose of top dressing is to protect the surface roots and avoid drying out, and also to discourage weed growth; the dressing assists the process of decomposition which provides plant food in small quantities just as it does under natural conditions. Once the plants become established they provide a thin top dressing from their own leaf fall.

Humus in the soil and on the surface is important to most heathers, as this is the natural condition in which they grow. All shallow rooting plants appreciate a surface dressing each year, such as granulated peat, pulverized bark, well-rotted leaf-mould made from leaves collected from trees growing on an acid soil, or bracken peat formed by the stacking and rotting down of bracken fronds. Garden compost should not be used, as this is invariably alkaline; mushroom compost, spent hops and farmyard manure are also all unsuitable for heathers unless they are very old and rotted down to a texture more like soil.

Sawdust and wood shavings are often readily available, and they are just as satisfactory as peat and the other materials mentioned provided they have been stacked outside for a long time and are well weathered (12 months is the ideal time, in my view). A dressing of fertilizer, applied in March, is essential both to feed the plants and to help with the further decomposition of the dressing. This process absorbs a great deal of nitrogen, and constant dressing with any humus materials over a period of years will result in deficiencies of nitrogen and other elements in the soil. Feeding with organic fertilizers, and the addition of trace elements as advised on pages 29–30, is important.

On reading the suggestions for looking after your heathers, you may doubt the claim that they make 'trouble-free' gardens. It is all a matter of comparisons. A little attention in the spring of each year, with trimming and feeding, and an annual top dressing while the soil is still warm in the autumn, will repay you with a garden needing the minimum of work and staying in excellent condition for many years.

Pests and Diseases

No genus of plants has fewer problems than heather. If a plant dies for any reason, apart from old age, this can invariably be attributed to being grown in an unsuitable soil, eg, lime-hating cultivars in an alkaline soil, or in conditions of extreme dryness or wetness. The plants can be damaged accidentally by people or animals, and young plants can be killed by dog droppings which, like all animal excrement, when fresh, is very toxic chemically to plant life.

Moles can undermine plants, causing them to dry out, or they may bury the plants in a mole-hill. Rabbits, deer and sheep can make a feast out of newly planted heathers in particular, but such damage amounts only to a severe pruning. After experiencing such attacks in three gardens, I found that in the long run the animals did me a favour and the plants benefited from the pruning. The main danger is to new plantings where the plants can be pulled out or their roots exposed; if not attended to quickly enough afterwards, they will dry out. Aphids and caterpillars have been known to affect plants, and the grubs of chafer beetles have sometimes caused damage to roots when a new garden was made out of old pasture.

Phytophthora cinnamoni, a soil-borne fungus attacking various plants, is a problem in many nurseries throughout the world, but a great deal has been done to overcome this. If you purchase healthy plants, and ensure good drainage, it is most unlikely to occur in a private garden. I have heard of alleged outbreaks of this disease, but the loss of plants attributed to it has invariably been the result of root-rot diseases such as *Pythium* or *Rhizoctonia*. These develop primarily as the result of unsuitable soil conditions such as waterlogging, or physical damage, which weaken the roots and make them liable to attack from the fungi.

Propagation

Seeds   Self-sown seedlings appear with a bewildering rapidity in an established heather garden, and it is equally simple to grow plants from seed sown in the spring in boxes. But heather seedlings rarely come true to the group of plants in which they appear or from which the seed is collected, owing to the cross-pollination effected by bees and insects. The majority of plants produced in this way have flowers of poor colour, although the plants are very healthy. There is a chance in a million that you may produce a plant with entirely new colouring, different habit, exceptional foliage and a totally unusual flowering time. It can be exciting to try, but you must be ruthless in judging those of merit and discard all but the most promising, unless you want a garden of wild heathers.

Seed should be collected in the autumn as soon as it is ripe, and appears likely to fall (early spring with winter-flowering cultivars) and kept dry until being sown thinly in early spring on a mixture of peat and soil from the heather beds. The mixture should be gently firmed in the box, but not compacted, and the seed scattered on the surface. Do not cover; water in with a fine spray. The boxes are best left outside in a shaded position and kept moist until the seeds germinate. Germination takes place over several years and is often much better after hard frosty conditions, so do not discard boxes too soon.

Layering   This method is the most reliable means of vegetative propagation, as the portion of plant being used remains as part of the parent plant until it is rooted and able to support itself unaided. It is ideal for producing the small number of plants needed in one's own garden. Quite apart from being reliable and producing a true reproduction of the parent, it also makes a plant large enough for planting out in one year and can be done without spoiling the existing plant. If you look carefully at established plants you will often find that branches in contact with the ground have formed roots, and the technique of layering is to assist the plant in doing the same thing on one or more stems. This is done by selecting long branches with plenty of young foliage and laying it down horizontally in the soil, leaving the tips exposed in a vertical position. It is simpler to use branches growing low down, but this is not vital as higher branches can be either pegged down, or weighted with a large stone or half brick laid on top. Choose healthy shoots and make sure that there is an acute turn on the layered branch; this retards the sap flow and is essential in stimulating root action. Then leave the layer alone for 12 months. Good rooting will often take place much sooner, especially on layers put down in the spring, and the work can be done at any time of year except when the weather is very frosty. A peat and sand mixture around the layer will help rooting, but is not essential provided the surrounding soil is crumbly in texture.

Cuttings   New plants that are identical to the parent can be raised easily by cuttings. The experienced amateur, or professional with modern aids to propagation such as mist, heated benches or special frames, can take cuttings all the year round. This may just as easily be done without any of these aids, provided the cuttings are taken at the correct time of year, which varies with the species. Cuttings of winter-flowering cultivars are usually best taken in June, before the following year's flower-buds are initiated, while those of summer-flowering types may be taken between August and October. Choose the non-flowering shoots of the current year's growth, when they are half ripe; they are then flexible and do not break easily. Cuttings taken in this way should be inserted in a mixture of 50% fine peat and 50% sharp lime-free sand in a pot or tray. Ideally, cuttings of 3 cm (1 in) long are taken and are inserted to half their length, the top of the tray is given a sprinkling of sharp sand and watered with a fine rose or spray. Do not compress the compost before inserting cuttings, and do not firm them in. It is far better to water them in afterwards and allow the watering to settle the compost. The pot or tray can be put into a shaded frame or greenhouse, or covered with clear polythene or a sheet of glass, and placed outside on the north side of a wall where direct sunlight does not get to it. If the frame, or box, is covered with polythene this prevents evaporation and will need little attention, but if it is uncovered, frequent spraying will be needed according to weather conditions. Seed trays with clear plastic covers are very successful for rooting cuttings.

I have found that late cuttings are equally successful if taken in the same way, and left in a cold frame for the winter, but this should not be in direct range of the sun in late winter or early spring. Most cultivars grown from cuttings will produce a 70% success rate and be ready for potting by April or May of the following season. This method is the cheapest and easiest of all and produces acceptable results for the amateur grower.

34

The Hardiness of Heaths and Heathers

In the British Isles all species of the hardy heaths mentioned in this book will grow successfully without any protection, although more than usually severe winters will cause damage to *Erica ciliaris*, *Erica vagans*, *Erica erigena* and tree heaths such as *Erica australis*, *Erica lusitanica* and *Erica x veitchii*, as happened in 1981–82.

Continental countries such as Holland and Germany are accustomed to more severe winters especially away from the influence of the sea. Enthusiasts protect any species or cultivar by laying branches of fir trees over the plants for the winter months. This most successful method of protection is worthwhile for anyone in a situation where the weather is more severe than normal, or where growing plants seem to suffer damage in average winter conditions because the garden is a frost pocket. The finest protection is a good layer of snow, but the weight of snow can cause damage to tree heaths and other taller cultivars by breaking them down. By covering plants too soon there is a danger that dampness will cause more damage than frost, and very often it is difficult to decide which species will suffer most, as many growers found to their cost in 1981–82 when normally tender or suspect species and cultivars came through unscathed and the so-called hardy ones were killed. Most of my continental friends ensure that they have young plants taken from cuttings and growing in frames as an insurance. They do not find it worth while to continue growing any species which is consistently damaged in the winter.

Descriptive list of Heaths and Heathers in Commercial Cultivation

In the following pages I have grouped together all cultivars in commercial cultivation at the time of publication. Each group is illustrated, showing my choice of one of the outstanding plants in each group. In case the actual plant shown proves unobtainable, alternatives are mentioned. You should be able to obtain most plants from any specialist heather nursery and a good selection from a reliable garden centre. To identify a plant which you already have, first identify the species. The illustrations on page 37 will help you to do this, as also will its flowering time. Once you have identified the species and colour of the flower, the names on the relevant page may remind you of the plant's label when purchased. At worst, you should be able to trace the plant from a small selection of names.

The general description of each species and its cultivation preference is given below.

Calluna vulgaris

The common Heather, or Ling, found growing on mooorland and mountains throughout the British Isles and also widely distributed throughout the world. All Callunas prefer to grow in a light lime-free soil with plenty of humus, and in an open sunny situation, but plants will be found growing well in a variety of conditions as long as the soil is slightly acid.

Daboecia azorica

The only native area for this species is in the Azores, and while it has similar characteristics to *D. cantabrica*, it is much dwarfer, and may be somewhat tender in the British Isles. Most plants grown under this name are hybrids but the true species can be, and is grown, flowering in May and June, approximately 15 cm (6 in) in height, and producing flowers varying from crimson to ruby. It is this plant that introduces the 'red' to the well-known hybrids. It prefers lime-free conditions and peaty soil.

Heather species (opposite): **A** *Calluna vulgaris*; **B** *Erica tetralix*; **C** *Erica cinerea*; **D** *Erica ciliaris*; **E** *Daboecia cantabrica*; **F** *Erica carnea*; **G** *Erica vagans*.

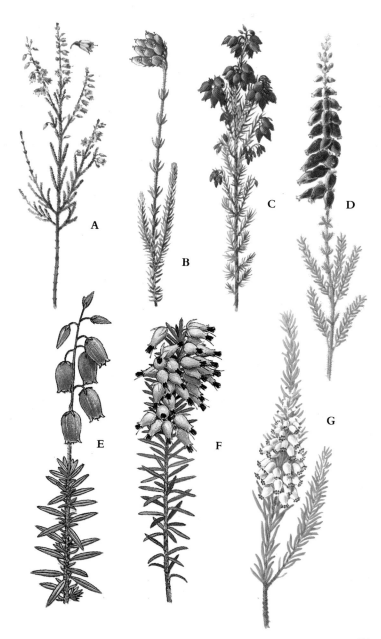

A

B

C

D

E

F

G

Daboecia cantabrica

St Daboec's Heath, found on moors in Co. Mayo and Co. Galway, and in northern Spain, Portugal and south-western France. In cultivation I have found it to be tolerant of drought and even alkaline soils. Flowered stems should be removed as soon as flowering has finished in order to keep plants tidy.

Daboecia x scotica
(D. azorica x D. cantabrica)

There are now a number of hybrids of this parentage, and also some back crosses as they are fertile, all of them being excellent garden plants of tidy habit, and fully hardy in the British Isles. They all remain very tidy even after flowering, when the dead flowers are most attractive.

Erica carnea

The Winter Heath, usually found with very heliotrope flowers in mountain areas of northern Italy, Yugoslavia, Albania, Switzerland, Austria, Czechoslovakia, southern Germany and Savoy. One of the hardiest garden plants in cultivation, flowering reliably during the winter, regardless of weather. All cultivars are tolerant of lime, but require the addition of peat if planted in excessively alkaline soils. Being very compact in habit they are good ground coverers and require trimming only every few years, if at all, and then immediately after flowering. The flowering season shown against each gives the times when some flowers are open; the main display is very much influenced by weather conditions, but is usually towards the middle two months shown.

Erica ciliaris

The Dorset Heath is found growing wild in Dorset, Devon, Cornwall and Co. Galway, and in some parts of France, Spain and Portugal. Summer-flowering plants which like acid soil with plenty of humus and plenty of sunshine. Although they prefer moist conditions they have done quite well in dry conditions prevailing in the last few years. Severe winter weather can damage them, but rarely kills outright. Careful pruning may be needed to prevent garden plants becoming straggly.

Erica cinerea

Bell Heather is a native of our own islands, and turns the drier moorlands into a sea of purple every summer. It enjoys a hot, dry position if planted with generous quantities of peat or other humus.

Generally it makes well-proportioned plants but the taller growing forms benefit from pruning as advised elsewhere. The flowering period is long—from June until November—and the colours range from pure white to deep ruby-red, with many attractive variations in foliage.

Erica erigena
Spring-flowering, lime tolerant species, all cultivars making very shapely plants taller than most, and very valuable as specimen plants amongst lower growing species as well as flowering in between the main winter and summer flowering season. I have found them to be quite hardy, but the taller kinds are brittle and may be damaged by snow.

Erica Hybrids
Under this heading fall the natural hybrids between differing species of Ericas. All are extremely interesting plants and, almost without exception, are hardy as they have inherited the good points of both parents. The winter-flowering forms must be considered as some of the best of all garden plants as they will tolerate the worst soil conditions, grow vigorously, flower freely unless in too much shade and require the minimum of trimming.

Winter Flowering Hybrids
The actual time of flowering is affected by the weather, but it is not unusual to find many of them flowering as early as September and as late as June.

E. x *darleyensis* (ie, *E. carnea* x *E. erigena*)

Summer Flowering Hybrids

E. x *stuartii* (*praegeri*) (ie, *E. mackaiana* x *E. tetralix*)

E. x *watsonii* (ie, *E. ciliaris* x *E. tetralix*)
In these hybrids the flowers tend to be like the *E. ciliaris* parent, but plant habit and arrangement of flowers vary between the characteristics of one parent and the other. All are very free flowering and compact in growth. With the exception of 'Truro', the original find in this group, all were collected in Dorset by the late D. F. Maxwell and his staff.

E. x *williamsii* (ie, *E. vagans* x *E. tetralix*)

Hybrid so far found only on the Lizard Peninsula, Cornwall. In my experience they have inherited the tolerance of indifferent soil conditions from *E. vagans*.

Erica mackaiana

A species found on the wet moors of Co. Galway and Co. Donegal, and in northern Spain. In the past often listed under *E. tetralix*, it is a distinct low-growing species performing well in lime-free garden soil.

Erica scoparia

This species is common in Spain, France and North Africa as a large growing shrub of little or no garden value, but forms are cultivated in this country.

Erica tetralix

The Cross-leaved Heath is a native found all over Britain, and north-western Europe, where it prefers the wetter moorland areas, but it will thrive in normal garden conditions where the soil is lime free. The flowers are normally carried over a long period in terminal umbels. I consider them as valuable garden plants for the grey foliage, which can be quite silver.

Erica umbellata

This plant originated in Portugal, southwest Spain and Morocco, and for this reason has always been regarded as doubtfully hardy in the British Isles, but it has done so well that the doubts are hardly justified.

Erica vagans

The Cornish Heath makes a well-clothed bush, equally attractive individually or *en masse*. It is usually found in the wild, growing either in southwest Cornwall or limited areas in western Europe on serpentine rock formations which are neutral or slightly alkaline soils with a pH of 7 to 7·5 in southwest Cornwall (5·5 to 6·8 in Ireland). This explains why this species does well on slightly alkaline soils, and on heavy soils where many of the other summer-flowering species are not too happy. In these conditions peat should be used generously to counteract excess lime, and improve soil structure. Flowering is generally from August until October, and the faded flowers which can be attractive shades of brown and russet make a valuable contribution to the winter scene in the heather garden.

Tree Heaths

Under this heading I have grouped together large heaths as is conventional in the heather world. Although they mostly grow in Spain, Portugal, North Africa and around the Mediterranean, they are generally hardy in the British Isles, suffering damage mainly from wind and snow which tend to break the plants. Even after such damage, hard pruning results in vigorous new growth from the base and quick recovery. All prefer neutral soil, but can grow in alkaline conditions. They can be planted in groups, but are mostly used as specimens for height, or against walls, and they usually flower when other species are mainly colourful foliage-wise, and fill a gap in the flowering season. The heights given are those attained in the colder areas after a few years. In milder parts such as Cornwall the size could be greater; on the other hand, in exposed areas, the size can be halved. The trials at Harrogate have shown this.

Erica arborea
Found from southern France to central Africa.

Erica australis
Grows wild in Portugal and southern Spain. The original plant offered by nurseries under this name has deep green foliage and rose-pink flowers.

In the wild, flower colours vary. Some have been recently collected, and it is probable that in time new and improved colour forms will be introduced.

Erica lusitanica
Found in Spain and Portugal, it is now naturalized in parts of France, Cornwall and Dorset.

Erica terminalis
Grows wild from southern Italy to southern Spain.

Erica x veitchii (ie, E. arborea x E. lusitanica)
Found on Veitch's Nursery at Exeter in the last century.

'Alba Elata'
August–October

White
50 cm (20 in)

The traditional 'lucky Scotch white heather' comes in many forms, and names, but from a garden point of view all serve the same purpose, and flower at approximately the same time. The lists below give the names of the cultivars in the tall and medium sized groups; the lower-growing ones are on page 50 under *Calluna vulgaris* 'Caerketton White':

Tall	'Long White'★	'Doris Rushworth'
'Alba Elegans'	'Lyle's Late White'†	'Drumra'★
'Alba Erecta'	'Mair's Variety'	'Eric Easton'
'Alba Pilosa'	'October White'†	'Herbert Mitchell'
'August Beauty'★	'Serlei'	'Janice Chapman'
'Beoley Elegance'†	'White Gown'†	'Kit Hill'★
'Braemar'	'White Queen'	'Pyramidalis'
'Cunneryensis'	*Medium*	'Shirley'
'Elegantissima'	'Alba Carlton'★	'Silver Spire'★
'Elegant Pearl'	'Alba Dumosa'	'Tenella'
'Hammondii'★	'Bransdale White'	'Torrisdale Bay'
'Hayesensis'	'Buxton Snowdrift'	'Torulosa'★

The cultivars I recommend as the best are marked ★. Those flowering later than usual are marked †.

'Alba Plena' (in foreground)   White
August–October   30 cm (12 in)

Heathers with double flowers are always popular as the blooms give added depth and flowering appears to be much more prolific. This form first appeared as a sport on a single-flowered cultivar and, from time to time, shows signs of reversion to single flowers.

A yellow foliage sport from this cultivar, 'Ruth Sparkes', is popular but also shows a tendency to revert by producing single flowers and green foliage instead of yellow.

Similar cultivars are 'Else Frye', of American origin, 'Isobel Hughes' and 'Platt's Surprise' which have arisen independently but are very similar in effect, and 'White Bouquet' which arose as a green sport on 'Ruth Sparkes' and is, strictly speaking, 'Alba Plena'.

All these have been largely superseded by 'Kinlochruel', a much more outstanding plant, shown on page 58.

CALLUNA VULGARIS

'Alison Yates'   White
September–October   50 cm (20 in)

Any plant, whether it is a heather or a plant of another family, is especially valuable in the garden if it combines excellent foliage which looks attractive all the year round, and also has good flowers. This cultivar has lovely silvery-grey foliage retaining its colour throughout the year and long white flower spikes appearing quite late in the season.

'Anthony Davis' is another very good plant of this type with shorter flowers which appear rather earlier. 'Silver King' is similar but not as reliable in growth, and 'Hirsuta Albiflora' and 'Tomentosa' are two old cultivars which flower very freely, but the foliage is not so silvery-grey.

'Allegro'
August–September

Crimson
38–60 cm (15 in–2 ft)

This recently introduced cultivar is the outstanding member of this group of prolific flowering 'red' Callunas. The plants are covered with flowers for six to eight weeks, making a fine show of colour. 'Allegretto' and 'Con Brio' are two even more recent selections which may prove to give a better display. 'Beechwood Crimson', 'Beoley Crimson' and 'Goldsworth Crimson' are tall cultivars with similar flower colours.

'Darkness' is a very popular, well-tried, more compact plant of the same type, giving a brighter overall appearance than several older cultivars of similar type, 'Alportii' and 'Alportii Praecox', the latter flowering two weeks earlier than the others. 'C. W. Nix' is similar in colour but the flower spikes are sparser. 'Carmen' and 'Ross Hutton' are both popular in continental Europe but have not superseded the others in Britain. 'Tenuis' is an old cultivar, popular as it is very low growing. It flowers in July–August, the overall colour effect being similar to the rest of this group. 'E. Hoare' is taller but less effective, 'Coccinea' has silver foliage but flowers sparingly, and 'Red Pimpernel', introduced recently, could become the best of the lower growing plants in this colour.

CALLUNA VULGARIS

'Barbara Fleur'   Salmon
July–August   60 cm (2 ft)

This has a colour shade unusual in the Callunas, with a stiff, upright
habit of growth, producing good flower spikes ideal for cutting and
flower arrangement. 'Hookstone' is a much older cultivar of similar
colour and habit, but the flower stem is not so thickly covered with
flower buds.

Several cultivars have been introduced with flowers more pink than
is usual in wild *Calluna* found on the moorlands, but the colours are
more lilac-pink than the clear pink of the two cultivars mentioned
above. All make attractive plants and have a quiet elegant way of
displaying their lighter coloured flowers. 'Grasmeriensis', 'Harry
Gibbon', 'Pallida', 'Pink Gown', 'September Pink' and 'Summer
Elegance' all share this quality without having the clear colour of
'Barbara Fleur' or 'Hookstone'.

'Barnett Anley'   Lilac-pink or mauve
August–October   45 cm (18 in)

This plant, and all those mentioned below and grouped with it, resemble the wild moorland Callunas in habit and flower colour.

'Barnett Anley' has a very good long, deep coloured flower spike, making it the most popular of its type in recent times, but all the others mentioned have good characteristics which I have summarized.

'Arina'—pale purple, clear green foliage; 'Balbithian Purple'—very compact; 'Betty Baum'—very free flowering; 'Carolyn'—very compact; 'Dart's Amethyst'—compact, with amethyst flowers, brighter than normal; 'Dart's Beauty'—bronze green leaves; 'Dart's Brilliant'—much taller, 60 cm (2 ft); 'Elegantissima Lilac'—bright green foliage, small flowers; 'French Gray'—spreading habit; 'Grizzly' and 'Serlei Rubra'—very vigorous and thought to be the same; 'Hollandia'—upright growth, good for cutting; 'L'Ancresse'—bicolor in bud, opening purple; 'Petra'—pale amethyst flowers; 'Purple Plume'—long spikes; 'Ralph Purnell'—very vigorous, long, deep mauve flower spikes and justifiably popular; 'Serlei Grandiflora'—very vigorous; 'Spicata'—probably the first selected form in commerce; 'Yvonne Claire'—an attractive, compact seedling.

47

CALLUNA VULGARIS

'Battle of Arnhem'
October–January

Lavender
45 cm (18 in)

Flowers are always welcome in late autumn and early winter. The pale purple flowers of this cultivar are most attractive and unaffected by weather conditions. This, with other similar cultivars, bridges the gap in the heather flowering season until the winter-flowering species open.

'Finale' is a very vigorous form, while 'Hiemalis' and 'Johnson's Variety' are very reliable and not so tall; 'Hibernica' is even lower growing, but it flowers a month or more earlier depending upon the locality. 'Durfordii' and 'Hyemalis Southcote' have much darker bronze-green foliage and are shy in flowering. 'Autumn Glow' and 'Saint Nick' are very successful in North America but do not flower satisfactorily in Europe.

'E. F. Brown', 'Frejus', 'Hilda Turberfield' and 'Tremans' are excellent plants, flowering two months earlier than 'Battle of Arnhem'. 'Walter Ingwersen' starts flowering in September and continues until December. Its beautiful, slender spikes are worthwhile in any garden.

'Beoley Gold' White

August–September 45 cm (18 in)

Heathers with golden foliage which keep the same colour throughout the year generally have white flowers. There are so many excellent cultivars that to make a choice of the so-called 'best' is invidious. Nevertheless, I still find this the most consistent in keeping its foliage colour throughout the year and it is very effective when in flower. Careful pruning to remove dead flowers after flowering improves the winter appearance.

'Gold Haze', 'Carole Chapman', 'Christina', 'Harlequin', 'Golden Max', 'Golden Turret' and 'Guinea Gold' all give the same garden effect as 'Beoley Gold', and all have the support from enthusiasts who think one or other is the best of its type.

'Cottswood Gold', 'Dart's Parrot', 'Karin Blum' and 'Marion Blum' are very recent introductions proving popular in Germany and Holland, where they are becoming more freely available than the older cultivars.

'Caerketton White'

White

June–September

Up to 30 cm (12 in)

Amongst the many white-flowered cultivars of *C. vulgaris* a few flower much earlier than the rest. All are fairly dwarf in habit, and the amount of flower can vary from season to season. This cultivar is the most reliable, but 'Alba Praecox', 'Corrie's White', 'Elkstone' and 'White Mite' serve the same purpose and are widely available.

There are also many other single white-flowered forms that flower at the more traditional time in August to September. They are very low growing in habit. Any of the following can be relied upon:

'Alba Minor'	'Calf of Man'	'Lyle's Surprise'
'Alba Pumila'	'Eshaness'	'Sandwood Bay'
'Alba Rigida'	'Glen Mashie'	'Scotch Mist'
'Balbithian White'	'Gnome'	'Sylvia'
'Ben Nevis'	'Laphroig'	'White Carpet'

'White Lawn' and 'Mullardoch' are very prostrate in growth, quite different from any of the above, but good plants for rock gardens. In addition, there are several very good white, compact, forms in the St Kilda collection referred to on page 66.

'County Wicklow' Pale shell-pink

August–October 30 cm (12 in)

One of the best double-flowered heathers, reliably covering itself every year with beautiful flowers. It keeps a compact habit, but careful trimming to remove dead flowers helps to improve the overall appearance when out of flower.

'Camla' is often regarded as synonymous, but there are plants offered under this name which have darker foliage, shorter flower spikes borne more upright than on 'County Wicklow', and which flower later in the year. From the point of view of effect in the garden, the plants are virtually identical.

'Radnor' is another excellent cultivar, on which double flowers of a very similar colour are carried rather more upright. 'Baby Wicklow' is a very dwarf sport from 'County Wicklow'; it makes a mound and has sparse flowers of similar colour and type.

There are a number of similar cultivars with deeper-coloured flowers: 'Carl Roders' is heliotrope, 'J. H. Hamilton' pink, 'Joan Sparkes' mauve, 'Jimmy Dyce' deep lilac-pink, and 'Red Favorit', a recent introduction, is deep pink and the richest colour of them all.

CALLUNA VULGARIS

'Cuprea'
August–September

Lavender
30 cm (12 in)

This was one of the first cultivars introduced, and popular on account of its attractive foliage; despite the increasing choice of cultivars now available, it is still justifiably popular. The copper-coloured foliage which deepens in winter, is unusual, the plants are very hardy and tolerant of damp climates, and while the colour is not so bright as that of some of its rivals, it is a very useful addition to a heather garden.

'Bognie' is similar, but lighter in foliage and flower colour. 'Spicata Aurea' and 'Terrick's Orange' both have similar foliage colours, with the added advantage that their new spring growth is much brighter for a few weeks.

'Inshriach Bronze' is very similar in winter, but goes through much more positive changes of foliage colour, from acid yellow-green in spring to rich gold in summer and copper colour in winter. I am very fond of this cultivar which, from the very large range available, is quite distinct.

'Dirry'   Lilac-pink
August–October   15 cm (6 in)

Plants of this colour have lost in popularity to those with clearer pink or 'red' shades. Nevertheless, there is a place in gardens for them, and many people still prefer them because they are closer to what is regarded as normal heather colour. This cultivar is of recent introduction and, despite its small size, produces a mass of very attractive flowers.

Some of the similar cultivars have flowers more 'blue' in tone, but the overall effect is much the same. I have chosen 'Dirry' because it produces a larger amount of flower than is the case with 'Argentea', 'Mrs Ronald Gray', 'Lady Maithe', 'Dark Sandwood Bay', 'Hester', 'Mauvelyn' and 'Rica'. 'Mullion', 'Kynance', 'Roma', 'Mizzen Head', 'Foxhollow Wanderer' and 'Penhale' grow taller, and make very effective ground cover in addition to giving a good display of flowers. The best of this habit and colour is 'Dunnydeer' with very large and densely packed flower stems.

'Darleyensis' is an old, but very distinct cultivar of similar colouring, but carrying its flowers in a most unusual curly-headed formation on the stem tips.

'Elsie Purnell'
August–October

Shell-pink
50 cm (20 in)

The taller double-flowered Callunas fully deserve the praises given to them, producing long, graceful flower spikes which give an excellent garden display, or can be cut and used for flower arrangements indoors. This cultivar is the lightest in colour, giving an overall effect as if it had a silvery sheen over it.

The even better known 'H. E. Beale' is very slightly deeper in colour, and the two are only distinguishable when grown alongside each other; there are deeper colours in the same habit of plant, which I have shown on page 61.

'Glencoe' and 'Applecross' are both offered in nurseries; their colour is much the same. 'Flore Pleno' also has a similar overall effect, but the flowers are nearer to lavender in colour. This cultivar was the first double sold commercially.

A recent introduction, 'Sonja', could upstage all its predecessors, producing shorter flower spikes very freely; the overall effect of this plant is quite outstanding.

'Golden Carpet'
August–September

Mauve
15 cm (6 in)

Its yellow foliage turns orange and develops red tints in winter; the plant makes a low hummock. The flowers are unimportant.

'Andrew Proudley', 'Bud Lyle', 'Dart's Flamboyant', 'David Hutton', 'Glenmorangie', 'Gold Kup', 'Hamlet Green', 'Hirta' (from the St Kilda Collection), 'Isobel Frye' (quite recently introduced and very promising), 'Jenny', 'John F. Letts', 'Lambstails' (with the delightful habit of new spring growth curling like a lamb's tail), 'Orange Carpet' (rather more vigorous), 'Orange Max', 'Purple Sandwood Bay', 'Salmon Leap' (most unusual with a salmon tinge to the foliage) and 'Soay' (also from St. Kilda) are all excellent plants, each with its own devotees. Given room I would plant them all.

'Multicolor' is distinct, because when well grown it is one of the finest of all heathers for winter foliage colour; it can be superb. Unfortunately there are poor forms of the plant which revert to green foliage and others that colour badly. If you can obtain the best form and give it a sunny, well-drained position in which to grow, it is a 'must'.

'Humpty Dumpty'

Mauve

August–September (if at all)

5–10 cm (2–4 in)

This is the most attractive of a delightful group of heathers which resemble a pincushion rather than heathers as normally seen. Forming a bright green mound of foliage, it also produces a few flowers, but they detract from the plant's appearance rather than improve it. The best way to grow and enjoy this cultivar, or a similar one, is to treat it as an alpine and grow it away from more vigorous plants that would soon swamp it. Good drainage is essential and garden refuse or other plant material must not be allowed to rest on the foliage.

Similar cultivars fall into two groups. The real dwarfs with few flowers are 'Flatling', 'Foxii', 'Foxii Nana', 'Harten's Findling', 'Pygmaea', 'The Pygmy', 'Velvet Dome' and 'Sedlonov'.

The more vigorous flowering forms are 'Californian Midge', 'Foxii Floribunda', 'Heideteppich', 'Heideberg', 'Heidezwerg', 'Hypnoides', 'Kees Gouda', 'Kuphaldtii', 'Loch-Na-Seil', 'Minima Smith's Variety', 'Minty', 'Molecule', 'Mousehole', 'Nana Compacta', 'Oxabach Carpet', 'Prostrata Flagelliformis', 'Startler', 'Gnome', 'Gnome Pink', 'Lyndon Proudley' and 'Tom Thumb'.

'Joy Vanstone'   Lavender
August–September   35 cm (14 in)

A foliage cultivar which retains a pleasing orange colour throughout the year. While the great majority develop very deep orange and red tints during the winter, this cultivar has proved the most reliable of those retaining lighter colouring. The flowers are also quite attractive, making a pleasing combination with the foliage, but the dead flowers do detract from the foliage colour in the winter and I recommend trimming them off.

'Bunsall' is rather smaller growing; 'Fairy' grows to 30 cm (12 in) and keeps a very tidy, compact habit; it is frequently offered in nurseries. 'Wood Close' is a nice, neat plant of similar height.

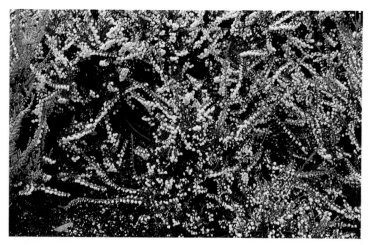

'Kinlochruel'   White
August–September   25 cm (10 in)

One of the most exciting introductions in recent years, this double white-flowered Calluna is outstanding because its white is so pure. It arose as a sport on 'County Wicklow' and Brigadier Montgomery who found it in his garden named it after his house. Forms originating as sports often revert, but I have experienced no problem whatsoever with 'Kinlochruel' which has proved to have a very good constitution, growing and flowering exceptionally well regardless of conditions.

'Kirby White'
August–October

White
50 cm (20 in)

I have always held plants in high regard when they give good garden interest for more than one reason, or at different times of the year. Obviously all the cultivars with yellow, orange, or other coloured foliage come within this category, and this cultivar is equally important in another way. In addition to having excellent white flowers similar to those of the traditional 'lucky Scottish white heather', the new spring growth is bright yellow; as the plant continues to grow throughout the summer, the bright tips are always colourful.

There are a number of cultivars with this characteristic. 'Ruby Slinger', 'Hugh Nicholson' and 'Loch Turret' are all very good and slightly smaller in growth. 'Hammondii Aureifolia', a much older cultivar, is excellent in the spring, but does not retain the foliage colour for so long through the summer. 'Alba Aurea', 'Alba Jae' and 'Spring Cream' are smaller in growth and good in the spring.

'Japanese White' is unusual in having foliage flecked with yellow splashes throughout the year.

CALLUNA VULGARIS

'My Dream'   White
August–November   50 cm (20 in)

A double white-flowered sport from 'H. E. Beale', raised by G. J. Cookes of Fenny Drayton. It produces long, elegant flower spikes, and makes an excellent garden display, as well as being useful for cutting for interior arrangements. This plant has been patented, restricting its distribution except through licensed growers. In my experience it has not grown well in the damp Lake District climate, and has shown a tendency to revert to the pink flower of its parent. A number of other growers have reported the same problem, but there is no doubt that if the conditions suit it, an impressive display will be given.

'Peter Sparkes'   Deep rose-pink

August–November   45 cm (18 in)

A superb plant with long flower spikes in a lovely colour much deeper than that of 'H. E. Beale' or 'Elsie Purnell' already described. If the garden is not large enough for all these cultivars to be grown in it, the selection must depend upon colour preference, as there is nothing to choose between them in other respects.

'Cramond', introduced in Scotland, is very similar in colour, but having rather shorter flower spikes it can appear to be a deeper shade. A German introduction, 'Schurig's Sensation', is also similar, but the overall effect can be a deeper colour.

Kurt Kramer of Suddorf has raised an even deeper coloured plant which he has named 'Annemarie', but this has so far proved to be variable in colour, the deepest colours being excellent. I am confident that within the next few years he will produce a true red double of a much deeper shade than has so far been seen in double-flowered Callunas.

'Robert Chapman'   Lavender
August–October   45 cm (18 in)

This plant is typical of many fine cultivars, having gold foliage in summer which turns to orange, flame and red shades in winter. Cold weather and hard frosts make the foliage brighter; sometimes it can be brilliant. Flowers are not important, but dead flowers should be trimmed off to improve the winter appearance.

As with other cultivars described earlier, it is extremely difficult to choose the best type, and all heather enthusiasts have their own favourite. Given suitable growing conditions in full sun, all the following will give excellent results: 'Amanda Wain', 'Arran Gold', 'Blazeaway', 'Bonfire Brilliance', 'Boskoop', 'Coral Island', 'Dart's Surprise', 'Dunnet Lime', 'Firefly', 'Fire King', 'Masquerade', 'Orange Queen', 'Red Max' and 'Richard Cooper'. In Holland, 'Boskoop' is the most popular; and in the last few years 'Dunnet Lime' has given the brightest foliage of all the cultivars in Germany.

'Roodkaptje'   Mauve
August–November   45 cm (18 in)

An unusual flowering form of Calluna in which the flower-buds never open as in a normal flower. On close examination a bicolor effect is seen, but the overall impression is mauve. The season for these flowers is long, and while they are in no way as showy as normal open flower spikes, they are nevertheless very attractive.

'David Eason' and 'Underwoodii' have been known for many years and are very similar in effect. 'Adrie', 'Dunwood', 'Evelyn', 'Ginkel's Glorie', 'Marilyn', 'Marleen' and 'Visser's Fancy' are all very similar, and all have their supporters. After growing them all for a few years, and seeing them on the Continent, I consider my selection to be the most consistent, but sentiment would persuade me to grow 'Ginkel's Glorie', which was found on Ginkel Heath in Holland where the airborne landing took place prior to the Battle of Arnhem. It was brought back from the Airborne Cemetery at Oosterbeek by General Urquhart, who was the British commander and is a heather enthusiast.

CALLUNA VULGARIS

'Rosalind: Underwood's Variety'　　　　　　　Lavender
August–September　　　　　　　　　　　　40 cm (15 in)

It is unusual to find Callunas which retain yellow foliage throughout the year and have flowers that are not white. An additional feature of this cultivar is that the foliage is flecked with orange and red in varying amounts throughout the season. This can be attractive on close examination of the plant.

'Rosalind: Crastock Heath Variety' and 'Serlei Lavender' also have yellow foliage with lavender flowers, but neither is so colourful foliagewise, as 'Underwood's Variety', nor have they the orange and red flecks in their foliage. Personally, I do not consider any of these cultivars so good, from a foliage point of view, as the white-flowered forms such as 'Beoley Gold'. However, for those attracted by the combination of yellow foliage and coloured flowers, this cultivar is the best to grow.

'Ruth Sparkes'
August–October

White
25 cm (10 in)

This is the only yellow-foliaged plant with double white flowers, and as a compact low grower, it is very useful. As mentioned on page 43, it is a sport from 'Alba Plena', and has shown an unfortunate tendency to revert to green foliage. A few years ago a reputedly non-reverting form was introduced and it was certainly an improvement. I have always considered that well-grown plants are less likely to suffer from this problem, and regular feeding and trimming will help to avoid it.

An exceptionally good plant with yellow foliage, and similar in habit, is 'Dart's Gold', but the flowers are only single. If a plant with small growing yellow foliage is required, regardless of the flowers, this latter could be the better choice.

'St Kilda Collection' ('Hirta')

This collection comprises plants found on the Island of St Kilda. Seventy clones of ling were collected there by R. J. Brien in 1965 and 1966, and 37 in 1980. After trials in Scotland and Holland nine clones have been named. All are dwarf and hug the ground. In the following descriptions the collection number is given in brackets.

'Alex Warwick' (K60), June–July; 10 cm (4 in); mid green foliage; white flowers. 'Boreray' (K70), July–August; 15 cm (6 in); dark green foliage, very compact growth, with long thin sprays of white flowers. 'Hirta' (K43), July–August; 7 cm (3 in); orange/gold foliage with new orange growth in spring; pale lilac-pink flowers. 'Minty' (K12), July–August; 7 cm (3 in); dark green-bronze foliage with some reddening at the base of the leaves; flowers pale lilac-pink. 'Mullach Mor' (K55), July–August; 10 cm (4 in); mid green foliage with excellent narrow-leaved laterals, and very long white flower spikes. 'Oiseval' (K52), 7 cm (3 in); foliage light green; white flowers with trailing habit. (K55 and K52 were selected as the best for Holland.) 'Soay' (K42), July–August; 10 cm (4 in); light bronze foliage turning reddish brown in winter; new spring growth pink, and red; lavender flowers; spread 25 cm (10 in) after 3 years.

'Silver Queen'
August–September

Lavender
35 cm (14 in)

Beautiful silver-grey foliage worthy of a place in any silver garden on an acid soil. As with all silver-foliaged plants, it needs well-drained growing conditions to give of its best; on wet sites it will prove disappointing.

The following cultivars are easier to grow and almost as good: 'Silver Knight', 'Oxshott Common', 'Beoley Silver', 'Dart's Silver Rocket', 'Glendoick Silver', 'Jan Dekker', 'Parson's Grey Selected' and 'Silver Sandra'. 'Pewter Plate', 'Silver Cloud', 'Silver Stream' and 'Grey Carpet' are all very low growing, the latter being much dwarfer than any others. 'Hirsuta Typica', or 'Hirsuta', are names given to the type of plant which, owing to common usage, has been associated with specific cultivars; the named cultivars are usually better.

Even more compact in habit, but with a similar type of foliage, is 'Sister Anne' which attains 15 cm (6 in) and spreads to 60 cm (2 ft); in well-drained conditions the downy grey-green foliage is very attractive. 'Chindit' is similar, but 'Dainty Bess' even smaller, growing to 10 cm (4 in). In America, 'Bess Junior', an even smaller form, is very attractive.

CALLUNA VULGARIS

'Silver Rose' Pale mauve

August–September 45 cm (18 in)

This plant relies upon a pleasant combination of silver-grey foliage and an abundance of flowers, giving an appearance of pink when fully out. While the foliage alone is not so attractive as that of 'Silver Queen' and other cultivars listed under that heading, it is, nevertheless, a good foliage plant and when in flower it is outstanding. In flowering time the large group in the garden of the Lakeland Horticultural Society at Holehird, Windermere, always makes one of the most attractive features. Despite the difficulties caused by spells of severe drought (even in the Lake District), or of extremely wet weather, its constitution is so good that it thrives regardless. 'Spook' is a similar cultivar, raised by Don Richards of Eskdale; it may well prove to be better than 'Silver Rose' but more time is needed for a true comparison to be made.

'Sir John Charrington'
August–October

Deep lilac-pink
40 cm (15 in)

A fine plant raised by the late J. W. Sparkes and presented to the late Sir John Charrington on his 80th birthday, in 1966, as a mark of appreciation for his work as a founder member of the Heather Society. The yellow-gold foliage develops orange tints, deepening as the year goes on, and turning red on all exposed leaves in winter. The colour of the foliage is more intense than in most cultivars of this type, and the flowers are certainly more 'red' in overall appearance.

'Late Crimson Gold', 'Crimson Glory' and 'Crimson Sunset' are all cultivars with a very similar 'red' flower colour, but the foliage is by no means so attractive. I have found that 'Wickwar Flame', 'Highland Rose' and 'Winter Fire' are very similar in habit with very good foliage colour, but the flowers are less good.

CALLUNA VULGARIS

'Skone'
August–October

Lilac-pink
45 cm (18 in)

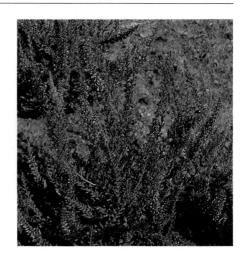

Several cultivars are selected for their interesting foliage because in it the normally green colouring is flecked with orange, red or pink. Other cultivars have small yellow patches on the otherwise normal foliage. The amount of colouring varies, and 'Skone' shows promise of being the most outstanding of its type.

'Naturpark' can also be very attractive, but it varies from one garden to another; I have seen plants equally good as the 'Skone' illustrated, and others with very little colour.

'Goldsworth Crimson Variegata' is the oldest of this type, but is usually flecked only very sparingly. 'Beoley Crimson Variegata', of recent introduction, is also less heavily flecked but has the advantage of the excellent long flower spikes of 'Beoley Crimson'.

'Rosalind: Underwood's Variety' (see page 64) is a yellow foliaged cultivar with orange and red flecks, and 'Japanese White' is one with yellow flecks only.

'Mrs Pat' has lovely pink new growth, but needs protection.

'Spitfire' — Pale mauve
August–October — 30 cm (12 in)

The foliage of this plant is unusual, in that the new spring growth has gold tips which turn yellow in summer, and it becomes bronze with red tips in winter. The plant tends to be ignored in favour of richer toned foliage cultivars that appear much showier, especially at the pot size stage. As with many older cultivars, it possesses a vigour and strength of constitution that makes it a much better plant for less favourable growing conditions. An established plant can be just as exciting as many that have supposedly superseded it, and most certainly should not be disregarded in planning a year round heather bed.

'Aurea' is very similar, being one of the oldest foliage cultivars grown, and is excellent. 'Glenfiddich' is a more recent introduction but by no means so good, in my experience.

'Ineke' is very much like these in summer with its yellow foliage, but instead of developing red tints, it deepens to a gold colour in winter. This one is at its most attractive in spring, when the new, light yellow growth appears.

'Spring Torch'
August–October

Mauve
45 cm (18 in)

One of the outstanding features in any spring garden is new growth on plants, and of this heathers provide many wonderful examples. The new growth appears in shades of cream, pink, red, orange and copper, like a torch, as its name implies. The effect lasts for only a few weeks, but is one of the highlights of any gardening year. There are many similar cultivars, varying in height from 25 cm (10 in) to 60 cm (2 ft); all are excellent but, in addition to 'Spring Torch', the most outstanding in my view have been 'Leslie Slinger' at 25 cm (10 in) and 'Fred J. Chapple' 50 cm (20 in).

Others of this type are 'Bray Head', 'Crowborough Beacon', 'Dart's Squirrel', 'Firebreak', 'Flamingo', 'Hammondii Rubrifolia', 'Mrs Alf', 'Olive Turner', 'Parson's Spectrum', 'Red Rug', 'Sally Anne Proudley', 'Skipper', 'Torogay', 'Tricolorifolia' and 'Hillbrook Sparkler'.

'Winter Chocolate' is slightly different in having bronze foliage most of the year and chocolate brown foliage in winter. As with the others, its main point of interest is its brilliant tips in spring.

'Sunset'
August–October

Pale lilac-pink
25 cm (10 in)

This cultivar is ideal where brightly coloured foliage is desirable, especially in the winter months. The difference between the similar cultivars is difficult to discern, but the most important variation is in height and habit of growth. Whereas those I have grouped under 'Robert Chapman' (page 62) have an upright habit, 'Sunset' and others listed below are more prostrate or compact. 'Sunset' is slow to establish, but once it has settled down its beautiful foliage is yellow-gold in spring, quickly developing orange and red tints in summer and very bright tints in winter. 'Golden Feather' has unusual long, featherlike stems.

As with many types of heather, all those listed below have their admirers; any specific comments I have to make are put in brackets. 'Glenlivet' (lower growing), 'Golden Rivulet' (long narrow growths), 'Gold Flame', 'Lewis Lilac', 'Llanbedrog Pride' (a sport from 'Peter Sparkes' with occasional double flowers), 'Parson's Gold', 'Prostrate Orange', 'Rannoch' (nice colours but not easy to grow), 'Roland Haagen', 'Rosebud', 'Springbank', 'Summer Orange', 'Sunrise' (rather more upright habit and a good contrast with its parent 'Sunset') and 'Talisker'.

'Tib'   Deep lilac-pink
July–October   25 cm (10 in)

'Tib' is the earliest double Calluna to flower, and one of the earliest of all the genus. This plant is covered with numerous long flower spikes which last for a considerable time. Whether or not one is making a heather garden, this cultivar will be most attractive in any floral display. 'Tib' was found on the Pentland Hills near Edinburgh by Miss Isobel Young and the name is the familiar form of Isobel in common use in Scotland. Heathers are often named after their finder, the place where they were found or people later associated with them; this is one excellent example of the first case.

'Ide's Double' is very similar, but taller in habit. 'Ingrid Bouter', a sport on 'Tib' originating in Holland, is rather darker in flower when the plant is seen in full bloom; individual flower stems are less dark.

'Alba Globosa' with 'Praegerae'   White

June–October   40 cm (15 in)

St Daboec's Heath is quite different in foliage from any other species. In cultivation I have found it to be tolerant of drought and also of alkaline soils, which is surprising when one considers its native conditions of damp, peaty soil.

The white forms are all excellent, and I have chosen this particular one because the bells are larger than those of the others. 'Early Bride' in the garden in Eskdale, Cumbria, where it originated, flowers earlier; 'Creeping White' and 'White Carpet' are much lower growing. 'Snowdrift' is a vigorous, free-flowering form, and 'Alba' covers a multitude of forms sold in nurseries. The plants do vary but all are good. 'David Moss' is a very good more compact form which grows to only 30 cm (12 in). It has excellent foliage, but in my experience does not flower repeatedly through the summer as do the others.

'Bicolor' Pale pink, purple, white or striped
June–October 45 cm (18 in)

A most interesting plant on which the flowers, even on the same stem, can vary: white, pale pink, purple, striped pink or purple on white. The calyx also varies in colour. The best forms of this plant can be very striking. There are many variations called 'Bicolor'. Quite frequently a planting of 'Bicolor' will contain plants with flowers similar to named forms mentioned below.

'Harlequin' is thought to be a seedling form with very similar characteristics. 'Cinderella' has white flowers with a flush of pink at the base, and is a delicate beauty. 'Donard Pink' and 'Pink' are often thought to be the same plant, with very pale pink, almost white flowers, but 'Donard Pink' has larger bells in the form that I grow, which came from Slieve Donard Nursery, Co. Down.

'Rosea' is frequently catalogued as 'white suffused pink' and, whatever its origin, it is virtually identical with 'Pink'. 'Globosa Pink' is a vigorous cultivar with dark green foliage and deep lilac-pink bells, and is unlike the other cultivars.

'Heather Yates'   Amethyst

July–November   30 cm (12 in)

The wild form of *Daboecia cantabrica* is usually lavender in colour and is a vigorous plant. 'Heather Yates' is a neat, compact plant with good dark green foliage and amethyst-coloured flowers which are very bright and effective. Two other selections from this colour range are 'Hookstone Purple', which is a larger and more vigorous plant of the same colour and 'Barbara Phillips', another excellent free-flowering form.

Deeper in colour, but not so bright overall, are 'Atropurpurea', 'Purpurea' and 'Rainbow' (which last I have not seen, but I understand it has a foliage flecked with yellow, and red variegations on the foliage).

Many plants with paler lavender flowers are sold under the name of 'Polifolia', but these are very variable, as each nursery selects its own form. A good colour cannot be assured unless the plant is bought in flower. 'Lilacina' is a good selected form, of fine colour and very free flowering.

'Porter's Variety'   Beetroot
May–September   30 cm (12 in)

This is a most unusual form of the species, with very dark green foliage, small leaves and small tubular bells of deep colour. It is not a good garden plant because it can be damaged in winter, and to flower well it needs plenty of water in the growing season. I have included it because it is so unusual in form and difficult to identify as a heather.

'Praegerae'
June–October

Deep pink
35 cm (14 in)

This is the best known of the pink forms as it has lovely glowing deep pink bells over a long season. It always flowers well, but its growth is rather untidy. Careful and quite hard pruning is essential to keep the plant trim. Such treatment is handsomely rewarded.

The colour of this plant is so attractive that several recent introductions have been made with similar flower colours and better habit of growth. 'Cupido', 'Covadonga', 'Waley's Red' and 'Wijnie' all have deep pink flowers, but I have seen only young plants of these cultivars, and their habit of growth cannot yet be judged. 'Blueless' has even clearer pink flowers, the colour of a plant in full bloom being less hard, but not quite so bright. The growth of the plant is more compact.

'Eskdale Baron' is another similar form.

'Tabramhill'   Deep crimson

May–December   20 cm (8 in)

There are a number of very good hybrids of the parentage (*D. azorica* x *D. cantabrica*) which have the dwarf habit and flower colours of the former, but have inherited the hardiness and long flowering season of the other parent.

This particular cultivar flowers earlier and remains in flower longer than any of the others, although 'William Buchanan' is the same flower colour and is better known. 'William Buchanan Gold' is similar, with red and gold variegation on the foliage; 'Jack Drake' is more compact with deeper-coloured ruby flowers, and 'Silverwells' is a lovely white-flowered form.

'Bearsden', 'Cora', 'Red Imp' and 'Robin' are all very similar to 'Tabramhill', but in my view inferior both to it and to 'William Buchanan'.

'Ann Sparkes'
Deep rose-pink

February–May
15 cm (6 in)

The winter flowering cultivars with colourful foliage are important because they belong to species which tolerate soil conditions unsuitable for *Calluna vulgaris* or *Erica cinerea*, the two species which provide most outstanding cultivars for foliage colour.

'Ann Sparkes' is slow growing and a very compact plant with yellow foliage in summer. This turns to bronze red in winter, as seen in the illustration. The flowers are a very good colour, taking after the parent plant 'Vivellii' from which 'Ann Sparkes' originated as a sport.

A very similar form introduced on the Continent is 'Vivellii Aurea', but in my experience this is not nearly so colourful or attractive. It is important to place 'Ann Sparkes' carefully in the garden, because it is so much slower growing than many of its relations, and can easily be overpowered by vigorous neighbours. However, it is such an excellent plant that careful cultivation will be repaid.

'Carnea'
Pink

January–April
20 cm (8 in)

The range of colours in winter-flowering heaths is rather limited, but owing to the size of flower, density of flowering, combination of flower and foliage colour, some cultivars appear much brighter in overall effect than others. When individual flowers of similar cultivars are examined, they may actually prove identical in colour.

This cultivar is an outstanding example, and the rich pink colouring of a plant in full flower is much brighter than that of many other cultivars.

'Alan Coates', 'Queen Mary' and 'Sherwood Creeping' (more often sold with the incorrect name of 'Sherwoodii') all have a similar colour effect.

'December Red' Deep lilac-pink
December–May 15 cm (6 in)

This name identifies an excellent plant with a spreading habit, long flowering season and good deep colour, but it rarely flowers in December, except in areas where the climate is very mild; and the colour is not red. When it was first introduced it was sold as 'Springwood Pink: dark form'; it is distinguishable from 'Springwood Pink' by its small dark green leaves and much deeper flower colour.

'Smart's Heath' was also originally named 'Springwood Pink: dark form'. It is very distinctive, with darker flowers and a blue-green tone to the foliage. Reputedly it flowers slightly earlier, but in my experience it is very difficult to know from one year to the next which of the *Erica carnea* cultivars will flower first, with the exception of the very early ones mentioned in the next few pages.

'Pirbright Rose' has always been a favourite of mine, with a good glowing appearance; 'Spring Cottage Crimson' sounds very similar, but I have not seen it.

ERICA CARNEA

'Eileen Porter'
October–April

Heliotrope
15 cm (6 in)

This lovely plant, which appears deep pink in full flower, is certainly the earliest, and has the longest flowering season of all. But it is also much more difficult to grow than some cultivars and is very slow. It should be given special care and attention and I suggest that it should be grown with 'Ann Sparkes', in a special place, rather than as part of a heather garden where it would have to compete with its more vigorous relatives. People often complain that it has suffered damage in hard winters, and is not fully hardy, but I do not accept this view. It is a plant of distinction which needs, deserves and certainly repays careful cultivation. I have found that it likes heavier soil and has responded very well to Lake District conditions, where it is growing more successfully than on lighter, sandy soils in the Midlands.

'John Kampa' is a recent introduction which gives a similar colour effect, and grows more vigorously, but it does not flower so early.

'Foxhollow'
January–April

Pale lavender
20 cm (8 in)

As the illustration shows, this is a superb foliage plant, light yellow in summer, deepening in winter. For anybody with an alkaline, or difficult soil unsuitable to other heathers, this plant is essential. The flowers are really insignificant. The importance of plants with colourful foliage has resulted in many similar cultivars being introduced since 'Foxhollow'; these vary minimally in colour, habit of growth or flower colour. 'Altadena', 'Sunshine Rambler', 'Westwood Yellow', 'Tybesta Gold' and 'Winter Gold' are all very good, but I have found 'Foxhollow' to be the most consistently healthy and colourful.

'Aurea' is the oldest *Erica carnea* cultivar grown for its foliage colour. Although it lacks the vigour and spreading habit of 'Foxhollow' and the others mentioned, I would include it in a collection because the flowers are a deeper colour and especially attractive in combination with the foliage. 'Margery Frearson' is similar, with deeper coloured flowers, and looks very promising.

'Jennifer Anne'
October–March

Pale lilac-pink
15 cm (6 in)

This cultivar has a long flowering season, starting to bloom very early, as does 'Eileen Porter', but the colour is paler and the plant more vigorous in growth. It originated as a seedling in my garden in the mid 1960s and was grown alongside all other *Erica carnea* cultivars known at that time. It consistently flowered earlier and for longer than any of them.

A cultivar called 'Early Red' was grown at Harlow Car at the time when the Heather Society Trials were starting. This was a reliable plant coming into flower well before Christmas, but I have never been able to trace its history.

'Winter Beauty' is an old cultivar and was certainly the earliest to flower in the original collection of cultivars offered before 1914. Unfortunately, many of the old cultivars became mixed up because they were all of such uniform colour. This cultivar in particular was mixed with 'King George'. The true 'Winter Beauty' is still sold and can be relied upon to flower before Christmas in the United Kingdom.

'King George'
December–March

Rose-pink
15 cm (6 in)

One of the greatest and best known of all heaths. It is completely hardy and is covered with flowers every year from before Christmas in mild weather. It is very compact, with dark green foliage.

My 20-year experience of growing all the cultivars of *Erica carnea* has convinced me that from a commercial point of view most of the older cultivars are mixed up; moreover, the way in which newer ones have been introduced has also caused confusion amongst them. While there are small differences in flower colour, flowering time and habit of growth, the garden effect of many of them is very much the same. My grouping is based upon my experience, and the ones I have illustrated are the most distinct and most freely available from nurseries.

'Accent', 'Beoley Pink', 'Hilletje', 'Gracilis', 'Queen of Spain', 'Pink Beauty', 'Rosy Gem', 'Rosy Morn' and 'Winter Melody' are all very similar. 'Lesley Sparkes' and 'Wanda' have flowers at the same time, and are similar in colour to those of 'King George', but their new growth is cream and salmon-pink. Close examination of the plants is needed to appreciate this very attractive characteristic.

'Loughrigg'
January–April

Rose-pink
15 cm (6 in)

Some plants are outstanding because the combination of flower and foliage colour is so good. Very dark green foliage which turns bronze, especially in winter, looks attractive at all times of year and sets off the prolific flowers extremely well.

'Heathwood' is very similar in both flower and foliage colour, but more compact in habit.

'Lohse's Rubin' is a recent introduction from Germany which looks very promising; the foliage is even darker bronze in colour.

'March Seedling'
February–March

Pale pink
20 cm (8 in)

One of the latest-flowering cultivars of *Erica carnea*, opening its very prolific flowers when many others are beginning to fade. This cultivar is easily recognized, as the large pale green flower-buds hang in clusters, giving a very attractive appearance even before flowering starts.

A cultivar sold under the name of 'Maroon Seedling' appears to be identical, the distinct name arising, as so often happens, from the misreading of a label.

Many of the old Backhouse varieties, which also flower late, with pale-coloured flowers, can be grouped with this for colour purposes, although they are rather different in habit with more upright growth. One characteristic which is shared by all later forms is the prominent green buds. 'C. J. Backhouse', 'James Backhouse', 'Pallida', 'Prince of Wales', 'Mrs Sam Doncaster' and 'Thomas Kingscote' are all much alike.

ERICA CARNEA

'Myretoun Ruby'
January–April

Heliotrope
20 cm (8 in)

The brilliant colour of this cultivar, which in overall effect is the reddest of all, makes it an essential plant for any heather garden, and it must have priority where only a few plants are grown. Dark green foliage and good healthy growth, with no weaknesses at all, make this the outstanding introduction of the last few years.

The original raiser of this plant wisely gave it to two nurserymen but, as has happened on other occasions, it was introduced under two names. The first, and correct name, is in the heading; the other name, 'Winter Jewel', is no longer valid.

'Pink Spangles'
February–April

Bicolor, two shades of pink
20 cm (8 in)

When the flowers open, and for some time afterwards, they are bicolored, with the corolla pink and the calyx the lighter shell-pink; but as the plant ages the overall colour becomes deeper pink. This is an extremely good plant, with plenty of vigour and numerous flowers. It was introduced in Cornwall by Treseders of Truro, and was originally thought to be *Erica* x *darleyensis* because of its vigour.

Very similar in effect, and equally good, is 'Foxhollow Fairy'; but when the flower is open the corolla is white and the calyx pink. The overall appearance is at all stages lighter than that of 'Pink Spangles', although the flowers do deepen in colour as they age. As the name suggests, this cultivar was introduced by John Letts from his garden named 'Foxhollow' at Windlesham, Surrey.

ERICA CARNEA

'Praecox Rubra'
December–March

Deep lilac-pink
15 cm (6 in)

Many gardeners disagree with the policy of replacing old and well-tried cultivars by new ones, in any species of garden plant, and it is remarkable how often the older ones return to popularity.

This cultivar, together with 'Atrorubra' and 'Ruby Glow', was the original 'red' winter flowering heath. It still fills an important place in the heather garden because it flowers earlier than the cultivars that have followed it, and are considered to have replaced it.

'R. B. Cooke'
January–March

Pale lavender
20 cm (8 in)

An unknown plant of mysterious origin that was sent to Harlow Car, Harrogate, to be included in the Heather Society Trials, and proved to be one of the star performers. The colour is undistinguished, but the overall effect is a pleasing pale pink, and the amount of flower is so dense that it stood out amongst rows of plants in flower, even where they were of stronger colours.

Since it has been introduced commercially, it has maintained its excellent performance and will probably take the place of 'Springwood Pink', which is similar in colour and habit. 'Winter Melody' is another new plant, which I have not yet seen, but from its description it appears to be similar.

'Snow Queen' White
January–March 15 cm (6 in)

Since the introduction of winter flowering heaths, the form 'Alba' has remained the only white one. This name covered many clones, some being good and others very poor. A good form is still grown in Germany and Holland, but in Britain 'Cecilia M. Beale', introduced by Maxwell & Beale of Dorset, became popular because it flowered well and was compact in growth. 'Snow Queen' produced in Holland in 1934 has always been popular because it has such a good compact habit, and flowers very freely. Where space is limited, this cultivar is excellent and preferable to 'Springwood White', shown on page 95.

In Germany, Kurt Kramer is raising hybrids between 'Snow Queen' and 'Springwood White', and by a process of careful selection intends to introduce a new cultivar with the best features of both plants.

'Springwood White'   White
January–March   20 cm (8 in)

One of the finest ground cover plants for any garden. The only criticism that can possibly be made is that it is too vigorous and needs trimming to keep it within its allotted place in the garden. Fine, bright green foliage, which enables it to be classed as a foliage plant, is covered in winter by clear white flowers with brown anthers.

The influence of garden centre type selling has resulted in the slower growing 'Snow Queen' becoming more popular, especially on the Continent, because it makes a better looking plant in a pot at the time of selling. The spreading habit of 'Springwood White' makes pot-grown plants look rather untidy, but for speed of growth and garden value it has no equal.

'Vivellii'   Deep rose-pink

January–April   15 cm (6 in)

This excellent plant with dark bronze-green foliage and attractive deep-coloured flowers is, for some inexplicable reason, not always easy to grow. Although I have studied failures in many gardens, there is no obvious reason why it does not flourish. I have grown it satisfactorily on very dry, sandy soils, and also in the wet climate of the Lake District; it did well on the heavy, clay soil in the Heather Society Trials in Harrogate.

A few years ago 'Adrienne Duncan' was introduced in Scotland. Although it is almost identical in foliage and flower colour, it is more vigorous and grows well for people who have failed to cultivate 'Vivellii' successfully. 'Urville' is sometimes thought to be a misspelling of 'Vivellii', but plants that I have grown and seen elsewhere are slightly different and inferior to 'Vivellii'. 'Rubinteppich', which I have not seen, is reputed to be similar, but more vigorous.

'Aurea'   Lilac-pink

August–October   30 cm (12 in)

'Aurea' is the only plant of this species with yellow foliage and its red tints make it attractive at certain times of the year. This is very much a foliage plant; the flowers are unimportant, and add very little to its attractiveness. Although *Erica ciliaris* has a reputation for being damaged in severe winters, I have always found 'Aurea' to be very hardy both in dry, sandy soils, and also in the wet conditions of Cumbria.

'Camla'   Lilac-pink

August–November   30 cm (12 in)

This is one of several named cultivars in which the colour of the flower appears pink overall, but has a mauve tone to it. This colouring is typical of the species normally found where it grows naturally. 'Camla' and the following cultivars are selections made either on account of their especially large flowers, or because they come from different geographical locations. 'Maweana', which is similar, was found in Portugal. 'Globosa' and 'Rotundiflora', which resemble each other, are also available in nurseries.

'Egdon Heath' is a pink-flowered cultivar which reputedly flowers earlier than any of the others.

'Corfe Castle'
August–October

Rose-pink
25 cm (10 in)

This excellent coloured form was found by George Osmond in the Corfe Castle area quite by chance, and I think it is the most attractive coloured form of *Erica ciliaris*. The flower-buds are a lovely salmon, opening to rose-pink, and this cultivar has proved to be very reliable in a number of different conditions.

Another excellent coloured form is 'Mrs C. H. Gill' which has darker foliage than normal, and crimson flowers. This cultivar has suffered damage from cold winds and, in my experience, is less hardy than the others.

'David McClintock'
July–October

Bicolor, white and
pink
25 cm (10 in)

This lovely plant was collected in Brittany by David McClintock, a
Vice-President of the Heather Society. As the buds begin to open they
are most attractive, their white bases tipped with deep pink. Sometimes
the flowers turn pink overall as they age.

'Wych' is an older cultivar on which the flowers are very pale pink,
and the tips fractionally deeper. 'Stapehill' is another normally regarded
as a white, but it has mauve tips. A very recent find by P. G. Turpin
the Chairman of the Heather Society and his wife has been named
'Cherry Turpin' after her. (First listed as *E. ciliaris*, 'Cherry Turpin' has
very recently been re-classified as *Erica* x *watsonii*.)

'Stoborough' — White
July–October   30 cm (12 in)

White-flowered forms of all species appear from time to time, and there is little doubt that many different ones have been, and are being sold as 'Alba'.

This cultivar was found by D. F. Maxwell near the hamlet of Stoborough in Dorset. He took cuttings of a plant with bright green foliage and large flowers which stood out like a beacon amongst the more usual pink *Erica ciliaris*. If this is well grown, it is an outstanding plant.

'White Wings' is white flowered and has unusually dark foliage inherited from its parent 'Mrs C. H. Gill'; it appeared as a sport on that cultivar. Unfortunately it has also an inherited tendency to be damaged by cold winds.

'Ann Berry'   Amethyst
July–October   20 cm (8 in)

The beautiful coloured foliage forms of this species are an essential part
of every heather garden if suitable growing conditions exist. Many
good cultivars are available, exhibiting foliage similar to that shown in
the illustration. Nothing is more certain than the fact that no two
heather enthusiasts will agree upon which of these forms is best, but I
have always considered 'Ann Berry' to provide the happier combination
of flower and foliage. 'Constance' which was propagated from a sport
on 'P. S. Patrick' is a good plant, but is not freely available; it has
beetroot-coloured flowers. 'Fiddlers Gold', 'Golden Hue', 'Golden
Sport', 'Guernsey Lime' and 'John Eason' are all similar in foliage colour,
but have slight variations in habit and flower colours.

'Cairn Valley'   Pink
June–August   20 cm (8 in)

Although less well known than some other cultivars of similar colour,
I have chosen to illustrate this because pink colourings in heaths
without a touch of blue in them are rare, and this is a very pretty
example of a clear pink colour. Many better-known cultivars serve the
same purpose in the garden, varying in colour from a deeper shade of
rose-pink, to a very pale shade of shell-pink. All are worth growing
and can be relied upon to give a good show. 'C. G. Best' is rose-pink,
'Frances' a little paler and 'Sandpit Hill' slightly paler still. 'Next Best' is
a sport from 'C. G. Best', with yellow markings on the foliage. At the
palest end of the colour scale, 'Janet' is the most delicate shade of shell-
pink. 'Pink Foam', 'Carnea' and 'Carnea: Underwood's Variety' are
similar, while 'Apple Blossom', 'Betty Macdonald', 'Blossom Time' and
'Duncan Fraser' are so pale that they are best described as white flushed
pink.

Attractive plants in the same colour range, whose colour is best
described as dusky pink, include 'Josephine Ross', 'Old Rose',
'Strawberry' and 'Guernsey Plum'.

'C. D. Eason'
June–September

Magenta

20 cm (8 in)

This cultivar must surely be the best known of this species; its colour is glowing and almost crimson. 'Callander', 'Hardwick's Rose', 'Lorna Anne Hutton', 'Michael Hugo', 'Mrs Dill', 'Mrs Ford', 'Pygmaea' and 'Startler' are all similar coloured forms.

'Rose Queen', 'Atrorubens: Rosea' and 'Son of Cevennes' are a lighter shade, while 'Splendens' as grown in Britain is also lighter in shade. In Holland it is regarded as synonymous with 'C. D. Eason'. The problem of having many cultivars so close in colour is that they become mixed up in cultivation. 'Glencairn' has the same flower colour, being a sport from 'C. D. Eason', but its new growth in spring is a very striking red. Although it does fade somewhat, the colour is noticeable throughout the year.

'Atrosanguinea: Smith's Variety' is a similar colour, but the intensity of flower and the very special luminous quality heightens its effect. Some recent introductions also have this quality: 'Stephen Davis', 'John Ardron', 'Brick', 'Bucklebury Red', 'Mrs E. A. Mitchell' and 'Providence' are all superb.

'Cevennes'
June–September

Mauve
30 cm (12 in)

The traditional colour of the heather moors is purple and numerous selections have been made over the years by nurserymen, and enthusiasts in colours ranging from lavender, through mauve to purple. This particular illustration could be of one of many, such as 'Hookstone Lavender', 'Lavender Lady', 'Lilacina', 'Lilac Time', 'Prostrate Lavender', 'Janet Warrilow' or 'Nellie Dawson'.

Very much paler in colour, and classified as lilac, are 'Jim Hardy', 'Lilian Martin', 'Pallida', 'Poltesco', 'Sea Foam' and 'Smith's Lawn', but these being rather pale and indefinite, are plants to be admired at close range, rather than used as part of a garden scheme.

'Schizopetala', 'W. G. Notley' and, more recently 'Yvonne', have botanical interest in that the corolla is split from tip to base into six segments. This gives a most unusual effect, but is not something to commend the plants in an average heather garden.

'Cindy'
June–November

Purple
25 cm (10 in)

The true purple colour is well represented in heaths, and in this species my choice would rest with either this cultivar or with 'Pentreath', probably because the foliage of both is very dark green, and the combination of old-fashioned Imperial Purple flower and foliage is superb. 'Colligan Bridge', 'Guernsey Purple', 'Joseph Murphy', 'Lankidden', 'Purple Beauty', 'Purpurea', and a recent introduction, 'Little Anne', are all good low-growing forms.

'P. S. Patrick' is taller, growing to 40 cm (15 in) and is a lovely plant of the same colour, but selected where height is needed in the garden. 'Grandiflora', 'Herman Dijkhuizen' and 'Pallas' are other taller forms that are all well worth growing.

'Eden Valley'
June–October

Lavender and white
bicolor
30 cm (12 in)

Bicolor flowers always have a special charm, and heaths are no exception. The white base and purple tips of this very free-flowering plant make it one of my favourites. It starts to bloom early in the summer, reaches a peak by August, but carries on producing new flowers for several months.

I have not seen a recent introduction named 'Harry Fulcher', reputedly an improvement; any plant with the same qualities as 'Eden Valley' is worth growing.

'G. Osmond', although not strictly a bicolor, has a very similar effect and is most attractive, the base being a pale lavender with deeper tips.

'Honeymoon' conjures up a romantic image and this very dainty plant with white flowers tipped in lavender is a specialist's item. It is very beautiful, but has far fewer flowers than the other cultivars and, not unexpectedly, a short flowering season.

'Golden Drop'   Mauve
June–August   15 cm (6 in)

This plant is grown for its foliage which is yellow in spring with the new growth, but soon turns to orange and a much deeper colour in winter. The flowers are unimportant. My experiences with the plant have always been good, but some people complain that it is difficult to grow. 'Rock Pool', 'Windlebrooke' and 'Golden Tee' have all been introduced as more vigorous forms, with the same, or a very similar colouring. If it will thrive in your garden, I consider 'Golden Drop' to be the best.

A most attractive little plant of similar colour, but very diminutive in stature, is 'Apricot Charm', and what a splendidly descriptive name it has. This is a plant to put in a special place where it can be cosseted.

'Katinka'
June–October

Beetroot
30 cm (12 in)

The deepest coloured form of this species, it is also the brightest, and has a lovely glow. 'Velvet Night', a very descriptive name, is excellent and easily available in Britain. 'Contrast', 'Ruby', 'Victoria', 'Violetta' and 'West End' are all very similar and worthwhile.

The colour is so deep that careful placing in the garden is important; a light background sets off the colour to good advantage. In the heather garden, I have always found the best background is a yellow foliaged *Calluna vulgaris*, so arranged that the deep coloured flowers are seen against the yellow foliage.

ERICA CINEREA

'Pink Ice'
June–October

Pink
20 cm (8 in)

This cultivar stands on its own because the flower colour is the purest pink of all, the colour, as the name suggests, of icing sugar or confectionery pink. It is not by any means the most free flowering or vigorous of plants, but it is very compact, has good deep green foliage which sets off the flowers very well, and it produces plenty of flowers for several months. I would be very reluctant to have a garden of heathers without it.

'Sherry'
June–September

Ruby
25 cm (10 in)

I have chosen this plant to represent that section of the species with what I call 'wine red' flowers. They have a rather less glowing colour than those of many cultivars in the 'C. D. Eason' group and are very beautiful indeed. The colour may not appeal to everyone; it is a matter of personal taste.

There is a large group of old, and more recently introduced cultivars of this colour, and the dividing line between it and others of similar colour is so close that distinction becomes very difficult.

'Atrorubens: Daisy Hill', 'Atrosanguinea: Reuthe's Variety', 'Coccinea', 'Foxhollow Mahogany', 'Glasnevin Red', 'Heidebrand', 'Lady Skelton', 'Novar', 'Penaz', 'Red Pentreath', 'Romiley', 'Rosabella', 'Rozanne Waterer' and 'Wine' are all very similar in overall effect, though close examination reveals differences. 'Joyce Burfitt' is similar, but its unusually small flowers give a uniquely dusky appearance. 'Fred Corston' and 'Tom Waterer' are rather lighter in colour, without being so bright as the 'C. D. Eason' group.

'Vivienne Patricia'
July–September

Amethyst
25 cm (10 in)

As a colour name the word amethyst conjures up for me a lovely glowing mauve, lighter than purple, but much brighter than mauve; and this describes the overall effect of this plant in full flower. Certain colours have a luminous effect and on a dull day stand out more than anything else. This description applies to this cultivar and also to 'Atropurpurea', 'Caldy Island', 'Miss Waters', 'My Love' and 'Newick Lilac'. Taller growing and very similar in colour, but less showy, are 'Heathfield' and 'Tilford'.

'White Dale'
July–August

White
25 cm (10 in)

Even in flowers, white is found in several shades. This cultivar, the 'whitest', is an excellent plant with very good habit and foliage.

'Aberfoyle', 'Alba', 'Alba Major', a dwarf form 'Alba Minor', 'Hookstone White' and 'Nell' are freely available, and make a good display. 'Rijneveld' has been introduced in Holland and is very highly thought of. It is fair to say that none of these would be a disappointment.

'Domino' is an interesting and most unusual white cultivar; its corolla is white, but, unusually, its anthers are dark brown. The rest of the plant, which has dark foliage, is more typical of a coloured flower form.

'Snow Cream' is another unusual plant where the foliage sometimes has cream, green or yellow shoots, but this habit is not consistent.

'Brightness'
March–May

Lilac-pink
40 cm (15 in)

This cultivar and the white form 'W. T. Rackliff' are the best known cultivars of this species. 'Brightness' is useful, as its flowering season extends well into spring. The deep green foliage and very tidy habit of growth make it an attractive plant out of flower. It can be used in a heather garden as a focal point to raise the height, or it can be a feature in a general border of shrubs.

There are several similar cultivars. 'Coccinea' is taller, but otherwise virtually indistinguishable. 'Glauca' has lilac flowers, 'Hibernica' shell-pink and 'Irish Silver' shell-pink with a silvery sheen. 'Nana' is dwarfer and rather less showy, and 'Rosea' and 'Rubra' are similar to 'Brightness' but paler in colour. 'Rosslare', which originated in a New Zealand nursery, is rather dull by comparison.

The tallest cultivar of this type is 'Superba', growing to 90 cm (3 ft) in most situations; in favoured gardens it can be 300 cm (10 ft) in height. This is a striking plant with shell-pink flowers and is often grown as a 'tree heath', but its vigorous growth makes it easily damaged by snow and wind, and careful pruning is necessary.

'Golden Lady'
May

White
60 cm (2 ft)

This plant is grown mostly for its foliage as the white flowers are very intermittent. In my own experience it has not flowered in, and does not enjoy the climate of the Lake District, but has proved to be successful in drier areas of Britain. It is very useful as an addition to any foliage plants that grow reasonably well on alkaline soils.

More recently introduced is 'Ewan Jones', with lime-green foliage and lilac-pink flowers. This is a useful foliage plant, contrasting well with others of the same species, but in the northwest it does not seem to be reliably hardy.

ERICA ERIGENA

'Irish Dusk'
November–May

Pink
45 cm (18 in)

This is one of the finest heaths introduced in the last few years. It has beautiful dark bronze green foliage, covered in deep salmon buds, opening pink. The flowering season is very long, and even in northern areas the flowers open before Christmas, regularly every year. The main display of flowers is from February onwards, but the plant is colourful for four or five months. In my view the quality of this cultivar is enhanced by a very happy combination of foliage and flower colour, and even out of flower it is so tidy in habit that it could well be mistaken for a dwarf conifer, and is a feature plant in the garden.

This plant was originally introduced as 'Irish Salmon', but the cultivar which correctly bears that name is more open in habit, taller, has lighter grey-green foliage, but equally attractive salmon flower-buds and pink flowers. I believe that most plants sold in the last few years as 'Irish Salmon' are really 'Irish Dusk', although the true 'Irish Salmon' is also sold.

'W. T. Rackliff'   White
February–May   45 cm (18 in)

An excellent plant with dark green foliage, making a rounded bush. The foliage is lighter in the spring, with new growth. In all situations I have found that it covers itself in white flowers every year and is quite justifiably one of the most popular of all heaths.

Various excellent white cultivars are available, 'Alba' being much taller with bright green foliage, 'Brian Proudley' also tall with long flower spikes and flowering much earlier, especially in more southern gardens. There are also smaller versions; 'Ivory' is strongly recommended by many, but I have never myself seen it. 'Alba Compacta' and 'Nana Alba' are cultivars of much longer standing, but nevertheless are well worth growing.

'Furzey'   Pink
January–May   45 cm (18 in)

Excellent dark green foliage, tidy, bushy habit, with the virtue of flowering well every year. An added bonus is cream, pink and red colourings in the new spring growth. 'J. W. Porter' is very similar but dwarfer in habit; the new spring growths are redder. 'Jack Stitt' is even smaller in growth, but the flower colour is deeper pink and the new growth very striking indeed.

'Darley Dale' is probably the best known of all the winter-flowering hybrids and is still sold as 'Darleyensis', although this name is no longer valid. The flower colour is pale lilac-pink, and although it has been superseded by improved colour forms, it is still an excellent plant. 'George Rendall', 'Ghost Hills' and 'James Smith' are all much deeper pink in colour; 'Erecta' is taller and more upright in growth, 'Archie Graham' is similar to 'Darley Dale', but a little deeper in colour. 'Jenny Porter' is a very pale lilac, so pale that it could almost be called white with a flush of lilac, and 'Margaret Porter' is lilac, again similar but a different shade. The tallest growing is 'Arthur Johnson', with beautiful long flower stems in lilac-pink, with a silvery sheen to them.

'Jack H. Brummage'
January–May

Heliotrope
30 cm (12 in)

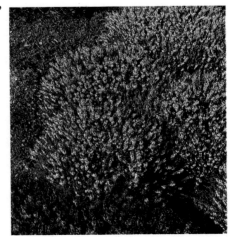

The only plant of its type that has coloured foliage all the year round. Yellow with orange, and with deeper gold tints in winter, it is most useful especially for those who cannot grow the more colourful foliage cultivars of species needing acid soils. I have always considered that it does best on richer, heavier soils, as it was always disappointing on the acid, sandy soils in my former Midlands home, and it is very slow in the heavier soil, but wet climate of the Lake District.

I have seen a plant in Holland, and once or twice in Britain, called 'Dawn Rogue' which appears to be very similar; but until I have seen a mature specimen it is difficult to make a positive judgment.

ERICA x DARLEYENSIS

'Silberschmelze'
January–May

White
45 cm (18 in)

Beautiful clear white flowers with light chocolate brown stamens in long spikes on dark green foliage are the features of this plant. As in most of these hybrids, the new growth in spring is creamy pink. The original plant of this particular form came from Germany, and it has received many names, some being translations into English; but the only English name now acceptable is 'Molten Silver'. You may well find this plant offered under either name.

There are a number of very similar cultivars, all excellent, but 'Dunreggan', 'Norman R. Webster' and 'White Perfection' have the advantage of starting to flower earlier.

'Ada S. Collings' and 'White Glow' are lower growing, and for many years were considered as cultivars of *Erica carnea*. Scientific tests are said to have established that both cultivars are in fact *E.* x *darleyensis* hybrids, but many will disagree.

'Irish Lemon'
May–September

Rose-pink
25 cm (10 in)

This beautiful plant is one of the outstanding introductions of recent years. Long before it begins to flower the new spring growth is a marvellous lemon yellow; the flowers are large and last a long time.

'Irish Orange' is a very similar plant, but the new spring growth has an orange tint to the basic yellow colour. Both these plants were found by David McClintock in Co. Donegal, Ireland, and were selected for the size and colour of their flowers. It was not until they were propagated and grown on in a nursery that the extra bonus of their beautiful spring foliage was discovered and they were given names.

This particular hybrid group was originally known as *E.* x *praegeri* and is a natural cross between *E. mackaiana* and *E. tetralix* which occurs only in Donegal and Connemara. The first plant collected was called *E. tetralix praegeri* (after Dr Lloyd Praeger who found it). It had magenta flowers and was subsequently given the clonal name of 'Connemara', when the hybrid status was confirmed. 'Stuartii' was a cultivar found in 1890 by Charles Stuart, and although the parentage proves to be the same, the plant is different from all others in that it has small pinched flowers which are pale pink at the base and very deep in colour at the tips. 'Nacung' is a more recent introduction selected for its much larger flowers.

'Dawn'   Lilac-pink
July–October   20 cm (8 in)

Large flowers are the main feature of this hybrid plant. It also has good spring foliage, when the new growth is red. One of the great advantages of most of the hybrids is their very long flowering season; in southern areas they may start to flower as early as June and will continue until late autumn.

The particular hybrid cross is *E. ciliaris* x *E. tetralix*, the original plant of this type having been found near Truro, Cornwall, by H. C. Watson many years ago. His find was listed for many years as *E. x watsonii*. The subsequent use of that name for the group meant that a clonal name had to be given to the original find, and this was 'Truro'. The first plant of this cross (*Erica* x *watsonii*) that D. F. Maxwell found and named was 'Ciliaris Hybrida'. This is still one of the most floriferous, and its new growth is bright yellow.

'Gwen', very similar to 'Dawn', is dwarfer, and its flowers are rather more lavender; 'H. Maxwell' is taller, and 'Rachel' more vigorous, with larger flowers. 'F. White', white with a pink flush, is less vigorous than the others.

'P. D. Williams'
July–November

Lilac-pink
25 cm (10 in)

This natural hybrid, found only on the Lizard in Cornwall, was first recorded in the 1860s but was not collected at that time. In 1910 it was again discovered by P. D. Williams, who took it into cultivation. Its spring foliage is yellow and it is attractive for most of the year with this colouring. The flowers are small, but very pretty. This particular clone was, and still often is, listed as *E.* x *williamsiana*.

'Gwavas' was discovered in 1924 by Miss G. Waterer, the finder of many fine heaths and heathers. Although the flowers are rather pale, a lilac-tinged shell-pink, the amount of flower makes up for this. I personally prefer 'P. D. Williams', but it is a matter of colour preference, as there is otherwise little to choose between them. Various other collections have been made from the same area of Cornwall, but I am told that in commerce they are indistinguishable from the two named clones.

'Dr Ronald Gray'
July–October

White
25 cm (10 in)

This lovely white cultivar introduced recently is proving very popular. Although it is less free flowering than for example, *Calluna vulgaris*, the bright green foliage is the perfect foil for the clear white flowers, and when out of flower the low-growing habit makes a most attractive ground cover.

The species described on this and the following page are less well known than most other heaths, but this white form and the pink 'Maura' are so attractive that they will soon become best sellers.

'Plena'
July–October

Magenta
25 cm (10 in)

The only truly double-flowered heath, this is the most attractive form of what is now confirmed to be a distinct species. For a long time *Erica mackaiana* was included with *Erica tetralix*. The original single-flowered plant was collected in Craiggamore, Ireland, by William M'Alla and sent by him to J. C. Mackay of the Botanic Garden in Dublin. This explains why the species is named *Erica mackaiana* and why the original single-flowered cultivar is now called 'Wm M'Alla'. 'Lawsoniana' is a much paler coloured single flower, 'Donegal' a larger flowered form of more recent discovery.

The most recent introduction is 'Maura', which has beautiful clear pink flowers without any trace of blue in the colouring. A most interesting introduction in northwest England is a double form, flowering much more freely than 'Plena'; it is called 'Ann D. Frearson'.

'Alba Mollis'
June–October

White
25 cm (10 in)

The combination of silver foliage and pure white flowers is always beautiful in any plant species, and heathers are no exception. If soil conditions are suitable (*E. tetralix* is the least lime tolerant of all heath species) this or a similar cultivar is indispensable.

'Bartinney', 'Melbury White' and 'White House' are very similar, and can be used for the same purpose.

'Hailstones' is a dwarf form, with dark green foliage, 'Alba Praecox' an old, but even earlier flowering cultivar, and 'Alba', as known in Britain, covers many white forms collected by various people. In Holland, plants grown under this name are the same as those called 'Alba Mollis' in Britain.

'Ardy'
June–October

Cerise
25 cm (10 in)

This plant has the reddest colour of all introduced clones of this species; and the combination of this lovely colour with the silver foliage common to the whole genus is delightful. In natural conditions *E. tetralix* is found on wetter moorland areas, but in cultivation it does well on drier soils provided they are lime free. In my experience this is the species most intolerant of alkaline soils.

'Foxhome' and 'Ken Underwood' have been well known for many years and are both still excellent plants, but its combination of flower and foliage gives 'Ardy' the advantage over both.

'Rubra' is the oldest cultivar of this colour, but by modern standards is insignificant.

'Con Underwood' and 'Daphne Underwood', although quite a deep pink, have rather more 'blue' in the colour. These are certainly better known in Britain, and very worthwhile garden plants. Personally, however, I favour flowers with a clean pink colour, and without the 'blue' tinge usual in heaths and heathers.

'Pink Star'   Pink
June–October   15 cm (6 in)

The wild species of the damp moorland areas are mainly pink-flowered, but there are many shades of pink. Some of the best colours have been selected and named. 'Pink Star' has attractive silver foliage and, being very compact in habit, carries its flowers on the end of the stem. It is my favourite.

'Darleyensis' has an unusual twisting habit of growth, 'Hookstone Pink' is the most vigorous and 'Allendale Pink', 'Helma', 'Humoresque', 'Pink Glow', 'Salmon Seedling' and 'Tina' are all typical. 'L. E. Underwood' is a charming plant with salmon buds, opening pale cerise; the effect is distinctly bicolor.

'Ruby's Variety' and 'Silver Bells' are off-white with a salmon flush and deeper tips.

'Mary Grace' and 'Terschelling' are a normal pink colour as in the wild form, but are unusual botanically.

'Afternoon' opens lilac-pink and as it ages deepens to heliotrope, which is an unusual characteristic.

Mauve

April–June

45 cm (18 in)

This species from Portugal, southwest Spain, and Morocco tolerates alkaline soils well, and despite it's origin has proved remarkably hardy in Britain. Beautiful mauve flowers with chocolate coloured anthers provide colour in between the normal flowering seasons, and it is surprising that it is not grown more frequently.

'Lyonesse' White
August–October 30 cm (12 in)

This is generally regarded as the best white of the species. Good solid flower spikes, pure white in colour, with golden brown anthers, are well set off against the good dark green foliage. In many of the alternatives the flower appears a creamy white rather than pure white, but close examination shows that this is often a matter of overall effect rather than of actual colour.

'Cream' has very dark anthers which affect the overall appearance and give rise to the name, but this strong, taller-growing plant is very effective, as also is 'Cornish Cream', the name in this case not being notably significant because virtually all *E. vagans* originate from the Lizard in Cornwall. 'White Rocket' is well named because the long flower spikes are very prominent.

'French White', 'Kevernensis Alba', 'Valerie Smith' and 'White Lady' are all more compact forms; 'Nana', as the name suggests, is much dwarfer but not free flowering.

'Mrs D. F. Maxwell'
August–October

Deep rose-pink
35 cm (14 in)

Considered by many to be one of the finest of all heaths in cultivation, it is certainly one of the best known. It is also a plant of the greatest possible merit if one takes into account the tolerance of this species for growing well in a wide range of conditions and on alkaline soils.

A number of others are very similar: 'Diana Hornibrook' flowering a little earlier, 'Birch Glow' having an even richer colouring. 'Fiddlestone', 'Miss Waterer' and 'Mrs Donaldson' are all much alike, but with a slightly different overall appearance in flower colour. 'Fiddlestone' has longer flower spikes, which seem to be a little paler in colour, 'Miss Waterer' has shorter flower spikes giving an effect of a richer colouring, and 'Mrs Donaldson' is more salmon in effect. However, the subtle differences in colour are apparent only when they are all grown side by side and started at the same age. Do not be afraid to grow any of them; they will all pay handsome dividends for the space they occupy.

'St Keverne'   Pink
August–November   25 cm (10 in)

Many pink-flowered forms have been introduced, but this cultivar is
quite distinct, having a clarity absent in all others. 'Hookstone Rosea',
'George Underwood' and 'Pyrenees Pink' are all very nice shades of
pink, the first named being deeper than 'St Keverne' but paler than
'Mrs D. F. Maxwell'; the others are both paler than 'St Keverne'. 'Peach
Blossom' and 'Summertime' are very delicate shades of shell-pink, and
both are compact growers.

Other so-called pinks usually have some varied tinge of blue in
them; 'Carnea' and 'Pallida' are both a rather washed-out pink, while
at the other end of the scale 'Rubra' is a very vigorous plant almost
mauve in colour. 'Grandiflora' with long flower spikes, 'Elegant Spike',
'Holden Pink', 'Ida M. Britten' and 'Lilacina' are all pink with a trace of
lilac, giving an entirely different but still attractive overall effect.

'Viridiflora' is a most unusual green-flowered form, regarded as a
botanical curiosity, but it could be much admired by flower arrangers.

'Valerie Proudley' White
September–November 15 cm (6 in)

The lovely bright yellow foliage is quite unique in this species, and given suitable conditions the plant is a gem. But I find it difficult to say what those conditions should be. I have seen it grow well on heavy clay soils in one place, and look very ill at ease in similar soils elsewhere; the same can be said of a wide range of soil conditions. It certainly needs full sun to show its best colour, and good drainage, and it must not be overgrown by any other more vigorous plants. My advice is to try it. The flowers are insignificant.

On numerous occasions I have been shown and asked to comment upon yellow-foliaged *E. vagans* which have appeared in gardens, causing the owners great excitement; but as soon as the plants are grown elsewhere the foliage turns to the normal green colour. For some reason this species appears to react dramatically to either the existence of, or lack of, certain chemical elements in local soil conditions. Fortunately, the foliage of 'Valerie Proudley' is consistently bright yellow.

ERICA ARBOREA

'Alpina'
March–May

White
120 cm (4 ft)

This form of *E. arborea* was collected in the mountains in Spain and is quite hardy in Britain. Tolerant of alkaline soils, it makes a fine feature plant either in the heather garden or in a shrubbery. 'Alpina' has very attractive pale green foliage, and covers itself in white flowers, which have a very slight scent. It is attractive at all times of the year.

The species grows in southern Europe, North Africa and parts of other countries bordering the Mediterranean, where it grows to 6 m (20 ft) or more, and is literally of tree dimensions. In Britain it is seldom more than about 2 m (6 ft) high, except in very sheltered areas where it will be taller. The French name for it is *la bruyère*; briar pipes are manufactured from its roots.

In commerce the larger and smaller forms may well be confused, as they bear the same name.

'Estrella Gold' White
March–May 120 cm (4 ft)

The ultimate height of this excellent golden foliage form is a matter of guesswork, as it has been introduced only recently. This cultivar was collected in Portugal by P. G. Zwijnenburg, the well-known Dutch heather specialist, and is proving to be very hardy indeed. It is an excellent plant.

At about the same time as this was introduced, an English enthusiast, Albert Turner, raised 'Albert's Gold'. Both this and 'Estrella Gold' are excellent, but similar cultivars, and enthusiasts are divided as to which is the better variety.

I have grown neither of them for long enough to decide on the merits of one against the other; but I already know that both fill a very important gap in the range of available heaths. It is unlikely that many nurseries will offer both, and I suggest that whichever you can obtain will please you.

'Riverslea'
April–June

Lilac-pink
150 cm (5 ft)

This particular cultivar was a seedling found in a nursery in 1946; it has deep green foliage and good flowers. The species grows in Portugal and southern Spain, and was introduced to Britain in 1769, its original colour being much paler than that of 'Riverslea'. Unfortunately, like all tree heaths, these are prone to damage by wind and snow, as the wood is very brittle and can be broken down easily at ground level.

Several seedlings grow on the rock garden at the Lakeland Horticultural Society's site at Windermere, Cumbria, and one of them is a very good deep pink in colour, giving an overall appearance of red when in full flower. This has been named 'Holehird', and I believe will prove to be the best form to date.

'Mr Robert' is a beautiful white-flowered cultivar with lighter green foliage. It was discovered in 1912 by Robert Williams in the mountains near Algericas in Spain, and sent to Kew Gardens by him. Unfortunately he was killed in action in World War I and as a tribute the plant was named after him.

December–April

White
150 cm (5 ft)

This tree heath which also comes from Spain and Portugal has now naturalized itself in parts of France, Cornwall and Dorset. In the southwest of Britain it grows to 300 cm (10 ft) and is used for the cut flower trade in white heather. As a garden plant it is good, although its hardiness is in doubt except in the more favoured parts of Britain. It will survive an average winter, but unusually severe weather is likely to kill it.

A most attractive yellow foliage form was raised by George Hunt and named 'George Hunt' after him. Although this plant seems to be flourishing in southern Britain, at Wisley, and elsewhere, it did not survive where I grew it in the Midlands or in the Lake District. This was the first heath to be registered under the Plant Patent legislation and George Hunt sold all his stock in aid of the National Cancer Research Campaign.

Thelma Woolner
July–October

Lilac-pink
45 cm (18 in)

This is a completely lime tolerant species from southern Italy and southern Spain, and is really a summer flowering tree heath. The deeper coloured form under this name was found in Sardinia, and is well worth growing, but the one most often seen in commerce is the paler coloured species.

'Exeter'
March–June

White
100 cm (3 ft 3 in)

This hybrid between *E. arborea* and *E. lusitanica* occurred in 1905 on the nursery of Robert Veitch & Sons Limited at Exeter. The growth and foliage are similar to those of *E. lusitanica*; the flowers, scented like hawthorn, are pink in bud and white when open. Sold as *E. veitchii* for many years, it was given the clonal name 'Exeter', as there are now several other forms.

For many years 'Gold Tips' was regarded as a form of *E. arborea*, as was also 'Pink Joy'. Both these cultivars have very colourful new spring growth, the outstanding feature of 'Gold Tips' being the gold tips on new growth. 'Pink Joy' has good new growth, but is most noticeable when its deep pink flower buds appear. When open they are white.

'Spring Smile' has been introduced very recently and this again has brilliantly coloured new spring growths. It is being listed as a form of *E. arborea*, but it is likely to belong to this hybrid group.

Index of Heather Names

The Heather Society is the International Registration Authority for heather names. All names that have been used for hardy heathers and have been brought to the notice of the Society's Registrar are included in this index. None of these names is therefore available for any other heather. It is a prime duty of an International Registration Authority to eliminate duplication; the list is also intended to form the basis on which the correct naming, spelling and orthography of all existing cultivars may be established. Because this book deals only with hardy species, none of the 630 or so species of Cape Heathers is included.

This list includes five groups of names:

1 Cultivars known to be in cultivation and available commercially. The names of these are·printed in Roman type and placed between single inverted commas. A page reference shows where each is mentioned in this book.
2 Cultivars known to have received their names since 1939, but which are not known yet to be commercially available. These names are printed in the same style as group 1, but with an asterisk against them instead of the page number.
3 Old names not traced as having been in use since 1939. These are also printed in the same style as groups 1 and 2, but are marked with the letter 'P' (Pre-war).
4 Botanical epithets. The boundary between these and the older names (group 3) is often obscure, and research is needed to establish their validity and application. Since they are all Latin specific names, they are printed in italics, with a small initial letter.
5 Synonyms, errors and misprints etc. These occur in all the four above groups. Each is thus printed in the style applicable to the group to which it belongs. The incorrect name appears first, followed by an '=' sign and the correct, valid name.

There are many difficulties in the compilation of a list such as this, and comments are very much wanted. These may be sent either to. the author, or to the Registrar of the Heather Society, whose address can be obtained from the Royal Horticultural Society.

Page references given in heavy type indicate where a cultivar·is illustrated.

CALLUNA VULGARIS

'Aberdeen',*
'Adrie', 63
adscendens
'A. G. T. White' = 'Beoley Gold'
alba
'Alba Aurea', 59
'Alba Aureifolia' = 'Hammondii Aureifolia'
'Alba Carlton', 42
'Alba Compacta', P
'Alba Dumosa', 42

'Alba Elata', 27, **42**
'Alba Elegans', 42
'Alba Elongata' = 'Mair's Variety'
'Alba Erecta', 42
'Alba Flore Pleno' = 'Alba Plena'
'Alba Gracilis', P
'Alba Humilis' P
'Alba Hypnoides', P
'Alba Jae', 59
'Alba Minima', P

'Alba Minor', 50
'Alba Minor Pumila' = 'Alba Pumila'
'Alba Multiflora', ★
'Alba Nana' = 'Alba Pumila'
'Alba Pilosa', 42
'Alba Plena', 27, **43**, 65
'Alba Praecox', 50
'Alba Procumbens', P
'Alba Pubescens', P
'Alba Pumila', 50
'Alba Rigida', 50
'Alba Robusta', P
'Alba Rubescens' = 'Alba Pubescens'
'Alba Serotina', P
'Alba Spicata', ★
'Alba Spicata Brevis', P
'Alba Splendens', ★
'Alba Stricta', P
'Alba Tomentosa', P
albiflora
'Albivariegata', P
albopurpurea
alboviolacea
'Albrechtii', P
'Alcester', ★
'Alex Warwick', 66
'Alison Yates', 28, **44**
'Allegretto', 45
'Allegro', **45**
'Almi', ★
'Alportii', 45
'alportii Coccinea', P
'Alportii Flore Pleno' = 'Flore Pleno'
'Alportii Late' = 'Goldsworth Crimson'
'Alportii Praecox', 27, 45
'Alportii Rigida' = 'Alba Rigida'
'Alportii Superba', P
'Alportii Variegata', P
'Alys Sutcliffe', ★
'Amanda Wain', 62
'Amilto', ★
'Amy', ★
'Andrew Proudley', 55
'Angela Wain', ★
'Anna', ★
'Anne Dobbin', ★
'Anne Gray', ★
'Annemarie', 61
'Anthony Davis', 28, 44
apetala
'Apollo', ★
'Applecross', 54
arborescens
arcticum
'Argentea', 53
'Ariadne', ★
'Arina', 47
'Arran Gold', 62
'Arthur Davis' = 'Anthony Davis'
'Arthur Pooley', ★

'Ashgarth Amber', ★
'Ashgarth Amethyst', ★
'Ashgarth Shell Pink', ★
'A. T. Johnson', ★
atlantica
'Atom', ★
'Atropurpurea', P
'Atrorubens' = 'Alportii'
'Atrosanguinea', P
'August Beauty', 42
'Aurea', 71
'Aureaefolia' = 'Hammondii Aureifolia'
'Aurea Pilosa' = 'Alba Pilosa'
'Aurea Pumila' = 'Alba Pumila'
aureifolia
aureo-variegata
autumnalis
'Autumn Beauty' ★
'Autumn Glow', 48

'Baby Wicklow', 51
'Balbithian Purple', 47
'Balbithian White', 50
'Barbara Fleur', **46**
'Barnett Anley', **47**
'Battle of Arnhem', **48**
'Bavelaw', P
'Bealeae', P
'Beechwood Crimson', 45
'Beleziae', P
'Beleziana' = 'Beleziae', P
'Ben Nevis', 50
'Ben Rhadda', ★
'Beoley Crimson', 27, 45, 70
'Beoley Crimson Variegata', 70
'Beoley Elegance', 42
'Beoley Elegans' = 'Beoley Elegance'
'Beoley Gold', 22, 28, **49**, 64
'Beoley Pink', ★
'Beoley Silver', 67
'Beoley Sport', ★
'Bernadette', ★
'Bess Junior' = 'Dainty Bess'
'Betty Baum', 47
bicolor
'Bill's White', ★
'Black Beauty' = 'Bronze Beauty'
'Black Forest', ★
'Blazeaway', 24, 62
'Blue Mist', ★
'B. M. Goffey' = 'Mrs B. M. Goffey'
'Bognie', 52
'Bonfire Brilliance', 62
'Boreray', 66
'Boskoop', 62
brachysepala
'Brachysepala Densa' = 'Darleyensis'
'Bradford', ★
'Braemar', 42
'Braeriach', ★

'God Pat' = 'Gold Pat'
'Golden Carpet', 28, **55**
'Golden Feather', 23, 73
'Golden Glory' = 'Golden Turret'
'Golden Haze' = 'Gold Haze'
'Golden Max', 49
'Golden Mrs Ronald Gray', ★
'Golden Pat' = 'Gold Pat'
'Golden Rivulet', 73
'Golden Rubra', ★
'Golden Tree', ★
'Golden Turret', 49
'Gold Flame', 73
'Gold Haze', 28, 49
'Gold Kup', 55
'Gold Pat', ★
'Goldsworth Crimson', 45
'Goldsworth Crimson Variegata', 70
'Goldsworth Pink', ★
'Gotteborg', ★
'Gracilis', P
'Gracilis Major', ★
'Graham's White' = 'White Lawn'
'Grampian', ★
grandiflora
'Grasmeriensis', 46
'Grayling', P
'Great Comp', ★
'Green Cardinal', ★
'Green Late White',★
'Gregor's Variety' = 'Macgregor's Variety'
'Grey Carpet', 67
'Greylag' = 'Grayling'
"Grimond' = 'Cramond'
'Grizzly', 47
'Guinea Gold', 49
'Gwenda', ★
gynodioica = diplocalyx

'Hamiltoniana' = 'Hammondii'
'Hamiltonii' = 'Hammondii'
'Hamlet Green', 55
'Hammondii', 42
'Hammondii Aurea' = 'Hammondii
   Aureifolia'
'Hammondii Aureifolia', 59
'Hammondii Rubrifolia', 72
'Hammoniae' = 'Hammondii'
'Happy Sam' = 'Braemar'
'Harlequin' ('Harlekin'), 28, 49
'Harpering', P
'Harris Tweed', ★
'Harry Gibbon', 46
'Harten's Findling', 56
'Hayesensis', 42
'Hayesii' = 'Hayesensis'
'H. E. Beale', 17, 23, 27, 54, 60, 61
'H. E. Beale Underwood's Variety' =
   'H. E. Beale'
'Heideberg', 56

'Heideteppich', 56
'Heidezwerg', 56
'Herbert Mitchell', 42
hermaphroditica
'Hershey's Late', ★
'Hester', 53
'H. G. Beale' = 'H. E. Beale'
'Hibernica', 24, 27, 48
'Hiemalis', 48
'Highland Rose', 69
'Hilda Turberfield', 48
'Hillbrook Orange', ★
'Hillbrook Sparkler', 72
hirsuta
'Hirsuta', 67
'Hirsuta Albiflora', 28, 44
hirsuta albo-rosea
'Hirsuta Albo-rosea', P
'Hirsuta Compacta' = 'Sister Anne'
'Hirsuta Incana' = 'Hirsuta Typica'
'Hirsuta Serotina', P
'Hirsuta Typica', 28, 67
hirsutior = hirsuta
hirta
'Hirta', 55, **66**
'Hollandia', 47
'Hookstone', 46
'Hortanulanus Janssen' = 'Frejus'
'Hostii', P
'Hubens' = 'Rubens'
'Hugh Nicholson', 59
'Humifusa', P
'Humils Compacta' = 'Mrs Ronald Gray'
'Humnel' = 'Minima Smith's Variety'
'Humpty Dumpty', **56**
'Hyemalis' = 'Hiemalis'
'Hyemalis Southcote' = 'Durfordii'
'Hypnoides', 56

'Ide's Double', 74
'Ignea' = 'Aurea'
'Ilka', ★
incana = hirsuta
'Ineke', 71
'Ingrid Bouter', 74
'Inshriach Bronze', 28, 52
'Islay Mist', ★
'Isobel Frye', 55
'Isobel Hughes', 43

'Jack's Favourite', ★
'James Hamilton' = 'J. H. Hamilton'
'Jan', ★
'Jan Dekker', 67
'Janice Chapman', 42
'Japanese White', 59, 70
'Jenny', 28, 55
'J. H. Hamilton', 27, 51
'Jimmy Dyce', 51
'Joan Sparkes', 51

'Mullion', 53
multibracteata
'Multicolor', 28, 55
'multiplex' = 'Flore Pleno'
'Murielle Dobson', ★
'My Dream', 17, 27, **60**

'Nana Alba' = 'Alba Pumila'
'Nana Aurea' = 'Cuprea'
'Nana Compacta', 56
'Nassau', ★
'Naturpark', 70
'New Sparkes', ★
'Nicola', ★
'Nivea' P
'Nordlicht' = 'Skone'
'Nudicapsula', P

'Oakham Common', P
'October Crimson', ★
'October White', 42
'Oiseval', 66
olbiensis
'Old Gold', ★
'Old Rose', ★
'Olive Cowan', ★
'Olive Turner', 72
omnium sanctorum
'Orange Beauty', ★
'Orange Carpet', 55
'Orange Max', 55
'Orange Queen', 28, 62
'Orange Sunset', ★
'Oxabach Carpet', 56
'Oxford Common' = 'Oxshott Common'
'Oxshott Common', 28, 67
'Oxtrot' = 'Oxshott Common'

pallens
'Pallida', 46
'Parsons Gold', 73
'Parsons Grey Selected', 67
'Parsons Spectrum', 72
parviflora
patula
pauciflora
'Pearl Drop', ★
pendula
'Penhale', 53
'Penny Bun', ★
pentamera
'Pentlandii' = 'Penhale'
'Pepper & Salt', ★
'Peter Sparkes', 17, 22, 24, 25, 27, **61**, 73
'Peter Sparkes Improved' = 'Peter Sparkes'
'Petra', 47
'Petrouschka', ★
'Pewter Plate', 67
pilosa
'Pilosa', = 'Alba Pilosa'

pilulifera
'Pink Beale' = 'H. E. Beale'
'Pink Fairy' = 'Fairy'
'Pink Gown', 46
'Pink Haze' = 'Silver Pink'
'Pink Spray', ★
'Pink Tips', ★
'Pixies Carpet' = 'Golden Carpet'
'Platt's Surprise', 43
'Plegance Pearl' = 'Elegant Pearl'
plena
'Plena' = 'Flore Pleno'
'Plena Flore' = 'Flore Pleno'
'Plena Multiplex' = 'Flore Pleno'
polychroma
'Polypetala' = 'Flore Pleno'
polysepala
polystyla
'Portugal', ★
praecox
'Praecox Tenuis' = 'Tenuis'
'Prairie Fire' = Multicolor'
'Prestwick', ★
procumbens
'Prolifera', P
prostrata
'Prostrata Alba', P
'Prostrata Flagelliformis', 56
'Prostrata Kuis' = 'Kuphaldtii'
'Prostrata Rubra', P
'Prostrate Orange', 73
pseudo omnium sanctorum = *terminalis*
pubescens = *hirsuta*
'Pubescens Alba', P
'Pumila', ★
'Pumila Rosea', P
'Punctata', P
'Purple', ★
'Purple Plume', 47
'Purple Sandwood Bay', 55
'Purple Sunset', ★
'Purpurascens', P
purpurea
'Pygmaea', 56
'Pygmaea Alba', P
'Pyramidalis', 42
'Pyrenaica' ★

'Radnor', 27, 51
'Rainbow', ★
'Ralph Purnell', 47
'Rannoch', 73
'Rannock' = 'Rannoch'
recta
'Red Carpet', ★
'Red Devon', ★
'Red Dragon', ★
'Red Favorit', 51
'Red Fred', ★
'Red Haze', ★

alba
'Alba' = any white flowered form; often incorrectly used as a name.
'Alba Globosa', **75**
'Alba Lutescens', P
'Alba Major' = 'Alba Globosa'
'Alba Stricta', ★
albiflora = *alba*
'Angustifolia', P
'April Fool' = 'Early Bride'
'Atra', P
'Atropurpurea', 77
'Atrosanguinea', P

'Barbara Phillips, 77
'Bicolor', **76**
'Bicolor Falso' = 'Donard Pink'
'Blonde' = 'Eskdale Blonde'
'Blueless', 79

'California', ★
'Calycina', P
'Calyculata' = 'Calycina'
'Candy', ★
'Cherub', ★
'Cinderella', 76
'Coccinea', P
'Covadonga', 79
'Creeping White', 75
'Cupido', 79

'Dark', P
'David Moss', 26, 75
'Donard Pink', 76
'Drummondii', P

'Early Bride', 75
empetrifolia = *cantabrica*
'Empetrioides', P
'Erecta', P
'Eskdale Baron', 79
'Eskdale Blea', ★
'Eskdale Blonde', ★
'Eskdale Maggie', ★

flore albo = *alba*

'Globosa Major' = 'Alba Globosa'
'Globosa Pink', 76
'Globularis' = 'Globosa Pink'
'Grandiflora', P

'Harlequin' ('Harlekin'), 76
'Heather Yates', 27, **77**
'Hirsuta', P
'Hookstone' = 'Hookstone Purple'
'Hookstone Purple', 26, 77

'Intermedia', P

'Lantern', ★
'Latifolia', P
'Lilacina', 27, 77
'Longifolia', P

'Maggie' = 'Eskdale Maggie'
'Minor', P
minus = 'Nana'

'Nana', P
'Nana Dumosa', P

pallida
'Parker's Variety' = 'Porter's Variety'
'Partner's Variety' = 'Porter's Variety'
'Pennsylvanica', ★
'Pink' = 'Donard Pink'
'Pink Lady' = 'Donard Pink'
polifolia = *cantabrica*
'Polifolia', 77
'Polifolia Compacta' = 'Heather Yates'
'Porber Crim' = 'Porter's Variety'
'Porter's Variety', **78**
'Potter's Variety' = 'Porter's Variety'
'Praecox', ★
'Praegerae', 26, 75, **79**
'Praegerae Alba', ★
'Praegerae Select' = 'Cupido'
'Pumila', P
'Pumila Stricta Alba', P
'Purpurea', 77
'Purpurea Globosa', P
'Pygmaea', = 'Nana'

'Rainbow', 77
'R. D. Broomfield', ★
rosea
'Rosea', 76
'Round', ★

'Snowdrift', 75
'Spire', ★
striata = 'Bicolor'
'Stricta', P
'Sweet Lavender', P

'Tricolor' = 'Rainbow'
'Tully', ★

'Varicolor' = 'Bicolor'
'Versicolor' = 'Bicolor'

'Waley's Red', 79
'White Carpet', 75
'Wijnie', 79

'Bearsden', 80
'Bit', ★

'Cora', 80

'Jack Drake', 80

'Mrs H. V. Manning', ★

'Praegerae Nana' = 'Jack Drake'

'Red Imp', 80
'Robin', 80

scotia = *scotica*
'Seedling No. 1' = 'William Buchanan'
'Seedling No. 2', ★
'Seedling No. 3' = 'Jack Drake'
'Silverwells', 80

'Tabramhill', 26, **80**

'William Buchanan', 26, 80
'William Buchanan Gold', 80
'William Buchanan Variegata' = 'William Buchanan Gold'

ERICA CARNEA

'Accent', 87
'Ada S. Collings' = *E.* × *darleyensis* 'Ada S. Collings'
'Adrienne Duncan', 96
'Alan Coates', 82
alba
'Alba', 94
'Alba Major' = 'Alba'
albida = *alba*
'Altadena', 85
'Amy Doncaster', ★
'Ann Markes' = 'Ann Sparkes'
'Ann Sparkes', 22, 26, **81**, 84
atrirubra = 'Atrorubra'
atropurpurea = *purpurascens*
'Atrorubens' = 'Atrorubra'
'Atrorubra', 92
'Audrey Morris' = 'Springwood Pink'
'Aurea', 85

'Beoley Pink', 87

'Carnea', **82**
carnea hybrida = *E.* × *darleyensis*
'Cecilia M. Beale', 94
'Cecilia M. Beale Pink', ★
'Christine Fletcher', ★
'C. J. Backhouse', 89
'Clare Wilkinson', ★
'Coccinea', P

'David's Seedling', ★
'December Pink' = 'December Red'
'December Red', 23, 24, 26, **83**
'Dommesmoen', ★
'Double Flowering', P

'Early Red', 86
'Eileen Porter', 27, **84**, 86
'Erecta' = *E.* × *darleyensis* 'Erecta'
'Ervillei' = 'Vivellii'

'Flore Rubro', P
'Fox Fairy' = 'Foxhollow Fairy'
'Foxfollow' = 'Foxhollow'
'Foxhollow', 22, 23, 24, 25, 26, **85**
'Foxhollow Fairy', 91

'Gracilis', 87
'Grandiflora', P
'Grof', ★

'Heathwood', 88
herbacea = *carnea*
herbacea hybrida = *E.* × *darleyensis*
'Hillbrook Pink', ★
'Hilletje', 87

'Jack Stitt' = *E.* × *darleyensis* 'Jack Stitt'
'James Backhouse', 89
'January Sun', ★
'Jennifer Anne', 27, **86**
'John Kampa', 84

'King George', 22, 23, 24, 25, 26, 86, **87**
'King George V' = 'King George'

'Lady Urville' = 'Urville'
'Lesley Sparkes', 87
'Lohse's Rubin', 88
'Loughrigg', 24, 25, 26, **88**

'Marchant's Crimson' = 'March Seedling'
'March Seedling', 23, 25, 26, **89**
'Margery Frearson', 85
'Maroon Seedling' = 'March Seedling'
'Mayfair White', ★
'Merton Ruby' = 'Myretoun Ruby'
'Miss Lynne' = 'Ann Sparkes'
'Mr. Reeves' = *E.* × *darleyensis* 'Darley Dale'
'Mrs Drummond', ★
'Mrs Sam Doncaster', 89
'Mrs Samuel Doncaster' = 'Mrs Sam Doncaster'

ERICA CILIARIS

'Egdon Heath', 98
eglandulosa

genuina = ciliaris
glabrescens
glandulosa
'Globosa', 98
'Globosa Rosea', ★
'Graham Stevens', ★
'Greyweathers', ★

'James Macluskey', ★
'Jean Liddle', ★

'Laxiflora', P

'Maweana', 98
'Mrs C. H. Gill', 27, 99, 101

'Nana' = 'Burfitt's Dwarf'
'Norden' = 'Globosa'

pallida
'Prolifera', P
'Purpurea', P

'Rodney', P
rosea
'Rotundiflora', 98
'Rotundifolia' = 'Rotundiflora'

'Stapehill', 100
'Stoborough', 27, **101**

'White Wings', 101
'Wych', 100

ERICA CINEREA

'Aberfoyle', 113
'A. E. Pearson' = 'C. E. Pearson'
alba
'Alba', 113
'Alba Compacta' = 'Alba Minor'
'Alba Grandiflora', P
'Alba Major', 113
'Alba Minor', 113
'Alba Multiflora', P
'Alba Nova', ★
'Alba Pallida', ★
'Alba Prostrata', P
'Alba Rosea', ★
albiflora
'Alfred Bowerman', ★
'Amaranthoides', P
anandra
'Angarrack', ★
'Anja Blum', ★
'Ann Berry', 27, **102**
'Apple Blossom', 103
'Apricot Charm', 108
'Ashgarth Garnet', ★
'Atrococcinea', ★
'Atropurpurea', 112
'Atrorosea', P
'Atrorubens', 104
'Atrorubens: Daisy Hill', 111
'Atrorubra' = 'Atrorubens'
'Atrosanguinea: Reuthe's Variety', 111
'Atrosanguinea: Smith's Variety', 104
'Autumn Pink', ★

'Baby Gold', ★
'Barnellan', ★
'Baylay's Variety', ★
'Betty Macdonald', 103
'Bicolor', P

'Black Knight' = 'Velvet Knight'
'Blood Red' = 'Sherry'
'Blossom Time', 103
'Boothii', P
'Brick', 104
'Bright and Beautiful', ★
'Broadstone', P
'Bucklebury Red', 104
'Buxton White', ★

'Cairn Valley', **103**
'Caldy Island', 27, 112
'Callander', 104
'Carnea', 103
'Carnea: Underwood's Variety', 103
'Carnescens', P
'C. D. Eason', **104**, 111
'C. E. Pearson' in Holland = 'C. D. Eason'
'Cerise', P
'Cevennensis', = 'Cevennes'
'Cevennes', 27, **105**
'C. G. Best', 103
'Champs Hill', ★
'Cherry Red' = 'Sherry'
'Christina Macdonald', ★
'Cindy', **106**
'Clevenessa' = 'Cevennes'
'Coccinea', 111
'Coccinea' in Holland = 'C. D. Eason'
'Coccinea Atropurpurea' = 'C. D. Eason'
'Coccinea Smith's Variety, P
'Coccinea Splendens', P
'Colligan Bridge', 106
'Collin Bridge' = 'Colligan Bridge'
'Constance', 102
'Contrast', 109
'Corsie White' = 'Hookstone White'
'Coy Spinel' = 'Foxhollow Mahogany'

153

ERICA ERIGENA

ERICA × DARLEYENSIS

'Ghost Hills', 22, 24, 26, 118
'G. Stevens' = 'Cherry Stevens'

'Hybrida Alba' = 'Silberschmelze'
hybrida darleyensis = *E.* × *darleyensis*

'Jack H. Brummage', 22, 24, 25, 26, **119**
'Jack Stitt', 118
'James Smith', 118
'Jenny Porter', 118
'J. H. Brummage' = 'Jack H. Brummage'
'Johann's Gift', ★
'John Wynne', P
'J. W. Porter', 118

'Knockomie' = 'Norman R. Webster'
'Knockowne' = 'Norman R. Webster'

'Loughrigg', = *E. carnea* 'Loughrigg'

'Margaret Porter', 118
'Molten Silver' = 'Silberschmelze'

'Norman R. Webster', 120
'N. R. Webster' = 'Norman R. Webster'

'Pink Spangles' = *E. carnea* 'Pink Spangles'
'Pirbright', ★
'Putford Pink', ★

'Rosea', ★
'Rosslare', = *E. erigena* 'Rosslare'
'Rubra', ★

'Silberlachs' = 'silberschmelze'
'Silbermilch' = 'Silberschmelze'
'Silberschmelze', 25, 26, **120**
'Silver Beads' = 'Silberschmelze'
'Silver Bells' = 'Silberschmelze'
'Silver Flower' = 'Silberschmelze'
'Silver Mint' = 'Silberschmelze'
'Silver Star' = 'Silberschmelze'
'Sjors Rendall' = 'George Rendall'
'Snowdrift' = 'Dunreggan'
'Snowflake' = 'Silberschmelze'

'W. G. Pine', ★
'White Form' = 'Silberschmelze'
'White Glow', 120
'White Gown' = 'White Glow'
'White Perfection', 120

ERICA × *STUARTII* (*PRAEGERI*)

'Connemara', 121

'Irish Lemon', 23, 27, **121**
'Irish Orange', 121

'Nacung', 121

'No. 1' = 'Irish Lemon'
'No. 2' = 'Irish Orange'
'No. 3' = 'Nacung'

'Stuartii', 121

ERICA × *WATSONII*

'Ciliaris Hybrida', 122

'Dawn', **122**

eglandulosa

'Flore Pleno' = *E. mackaiana* 'Plena'
'F. White', 122

glandulosa
'Gwen', 122

'H. Maxwell', 122

'Morning Glow' = 'F. White'

'Rachel', 122

'Truro', 39, 122

waltonii = *watsonii*

ERICA × *WILLIAMSII*

'Gwavas', 123

'P. D. Williams', **123**

ERICA MACKAIANA

'Ann D. Frearson', 125

'Maura', 124, 125

'Carnea', P
'Crawfordii' = 'Plena'

'Plena', **125**
pleniflora = 'Plena'

'Dawn' = *E.* × *watsonii* 'Dawn'
'Donegal', 125
'Dr. Ronald Gray', **124**

'Rubra', P

watsonii = *E.* × *watsonii*

'Lawsoniana', 125

'Wm M'Alla', 125

ERICA SCOPARIA

azorica

'Minima', ★
'Minor' = 'Minima'

chlorantha
compacta = 'Minima'
congesta = *azorica*

'Nana' = 'Minima'

erythrata

parviflora = *azorica*
platycodon

'Lionel Woolner', ★

portosancto
'Pumila' = 'minima'

'Mercedes Gold', ★

purpurascens

ERICA TETRALIX

'Afternoon', 128
'Alba', 126
'Alba Major', P
'Alba Mollis', **126**
'Alba Praecox', 126
'Alb. Moles' = 'Alba Mollis'
'Allendale Pink', 128
alpina
anadra
'Ardy', **127**
assoi
'Aurea', ★

'Bala', ★
'Bartinney', 126
'Bicolor', P
'Bury's Variety' = 'Ruby's Variety'

'Caerulea, P
'Candel', P
canescens
'Canescens Alba', P
'Carnea', P
'Carnosa', P
'Coccinea', P
'Commander L. E. Underwood' = 'L. E. Underwood'
'Connie Underwood' = 'Con Underwood'
'Constance Underwood' = 'Con Underwood'

contracta
'Con Underwood', 24, 26, 127
'Crawfordii' = *E. mackaiana* 'Plena'

'Daphne Underwood', 127
'Darleyensis' 128
'Delta', ★
'Denmark', ★

eciliata
eglandulosa
'Eric Birse', ★

'Findling Deimern', ★
fissa
'Foxhome', 127
fucescens

'Galway', ★
genuina = *tetralix*
'George Frazer', ★
'George Frazier', = 'George Frazer'
glabrescens
glandulosa
'Gratis', ★

'Hailstones', 126
'Helma', 128
'Hookstone Pink', 25, 128
'Humoresque', 128

'Intermedia', P

'Jean Liddle' = *E. ciliaris* 'Jean Liddle'

'Ken Underwood', 127

latifolia
'Lawsoniana' = *E. mackaiana* 'Lawsoniana'
'L. E. Underwood', 128
'Linford', ★

mackayi = *E. mackaiana*
'Mackayi Plena' = *E. mackaiana* 'Plena'
'Major Pallido', P
'Martiana Plena' = *E. mackaiana* 'Plena'
martinesii
'Mary Grace', 128
'Melbury White', 23, 26, 126
'Minor', P
'Molle' = 'Alba Mollis'
mollis
'Morning Glow' = *E. × watsonii*
  'F. White'
'Mrs Gill' = *E. ciliaris* 'Mrs C. H. Gill'

'October Crimson', ★

'Pallida', P
parviflora
'Pearls', ★
'Pink Carpet', ★
'Pink Glow', 128
'Pink Star', 22, 26, **128**
'Pink Tipped' = 'Sunrise' = *E. × watsonii*
  'F. White'
'Plena' = *E. mackaiana* 'Plena'
pleniflora = *E. mackaiana* 'Plena'
'Praecox', P

'Praecox Alba Mollis' = 'Alba Mollis'
'Praegeri' = *E. × praegeri*
'Purpurea', P
'Pygmaea Alba', P

quinaria

racemosa
'Rosea', ★
'Rubescens', P
'Rubra', 127
'Ruby' = 'Ruby's Variety'
'Ruby's Select' = 'Ruby's Variety'
'Ruby's Variety', 128
'Rufus', ★
'Ruth's Gold', ★

'St Nicholas' = 'Alba Mollis'
'Salmon Seedling', 128
'Shetland Island', ★
'Silver Bells', 128
'Speciosa', P
'Stardom', ★
'Sunrise' = *E. × watsonii* 'F. White'

'Terschelling', 128
'Thule White' = 'Hailstones'
'Tina', 128
tomentosa

verinensis
'Violacea', P
vulgaris = *tetralix*

watsonii = *E. × watsonii*
'White House', 126
'William Sloan', ★

ERICA UMBELLATA, 26, **129**

anandra
filifolia
major

subcampanulata
subcapitata

ERICA VAGANS

alba
'Alba Minima' = 'Alba Nana'
'Alba Minor' = 'Alba Nana'
'Alba Multiflora', P
'Alba Nana', ★
'Alba Superba Darleyensis' = 'Cream'
'Alba Tenella', P
albiflora = *alba*
anandra

'Birch Glow', 131
'Buchantha', P

campanulata
'Capitata', P
'Carnea', 132
'Catherine Graham', P
'Chittenden', P
'Coccinea', ★

'Colstoun Variety', ★
'Cornish Cream', 130
'Cream', 130
'Creamy Spire' = 'Cream'

decipiens
'Diana Hornibrook', 27, 131

'Early Pink', ★
'Elegant Spike', 132

'Fiddlestone', 131
flore pleno
'Floribunda', P
'French White', 130

'George Underwood', 132
'Grandiflora', 132

'Holden Pink', 132
'Hookstone Rose' = 'Hookstone Rosea'
'Hookstone Rosea', 132

'Ida M. Britten', 132
'Intermedia', P

'J. C. Fletcher', ★
'J. W. Porter', ★

kevernensis = 'St. Keverne',
'Kevernensis Alba', 130

'Latin Dancer' = 'White Dancer'
'Leucantha', ★
'Lilacina', 132
'Lyonesse', 24, 25, 27, **130**

'Minima', P
'Minor', P
'Minor Pallens', P
'Miss Waterer', 131
'Mrs Brittain' = 'Ida M. Britten'

'Mrs D. F. Maxwell', 22, 23, 24, 25, 27, **131**, 132
'Mrs Donaldson', 131
'Mrs Maxwell (of Doncaster), P
'Mullion', ★
'Multiflora', ★
'Multiflora Grandiflora' = 'Grandiflora'

nana = 'Alba Nana'
'Nana', 130

'Old Rose', ★

'Pallida', 132
parviflora
'Peach Blossom', 132
purpurascens
purpurea
'Pyrenees Pink', 132
'Pyrenees White', ★

reflexa
'Rosea', ★
rubens
'Rubra', 132
'Rubra Grandiflora', P

'St Keverne', 22, 23, 24, 27, **132**
'Summertime', 132
'Summer White', ★

'Tenella', ★
tubulosa

'Valerie Proudley', **133**
'Valerie Smith', 130
verticiliata = *E. manipuliflora*
'Viridiflora', 132

'White Dancer', ★
'White Lady', 130
'White Rocket', 130
'White Spire', ★

ERICA ARBOREA

'Alba', ★
albae
'Albert's Gold', 135
albida
'Alpina', 10, 22, **134**
'Alpine Gold' = 'Albert's Gold'
asturea

'Carnea', P
'Chelsea Time', ★
chlorantha
clarae

elii
erythrosigma
'Estrella Gold', 23, **135**

flore carneo

gallifera
genuina = *arborea*
glabriuscula
'Gold Tips' = *E.* × *veitchii* 'Gold Tips'
grandiflora

helenae

leptophylla
longistyla

mauritanica
'Minima', P
'Montana' = 'Alpina'

'Nana', P

occidentalis = *arborea*
odorata
'Oratava', ★

parviflora
'Picos Pygmy', ★

'Pink Tips' = E. × *veitchii* 'Pink Joy'
'Plena' = 'Alpina'

'Racemosa', ★
ramosa
riojana
rupestris

saccata
'Spring Smile' = E. × *veitchii* 'Spring Smile'
squarrosa
stylosa
'Suarcolens',★

trinitatis
typica = *arborea*

'Woolner's Gold', ★

ERICA AUSTRALIS

albiflora
aragonensis

bethurica

'Castellar Blush',★
'Castellar Garnet',★

'Dolinside Seedling',★

'Holehird', 136

'Mount Stewart', P
'Mr Robert', 136

'Nana', P

'Riverslea', **136**
'Roundhill', P
'Rubra', P

'Superba', P

'Wishanger Pink', ★

ERICA LUSITANICA, **137**

E. *codonodes* = E. *lusitanica*

'George Hunt', 137

'Lionel Fortescue' = E. *lusitanica*
'Louise Fortescue' = 'Lionel Fortescue'

ERICA TERMINALIS

albiflora

brevifolia

corsica = E. *terminalis*

flore albo = *albiflora*

'Hidcote Variety', ★

longifolia

ramulosa
'Ramulosa Major', P

'Stricta' = E. *terminalis*

'Thelma Woolner', 22, **138**

vulgaris = E. *terminalis*

ERICA × VEITCHII

'Exeter', **139**
'Gold Tips', 139
'Pink Joy', 139

'Spring Smile', 139

veitchiana = *veitchii*
veithchii = *veitchii*